Better Homes and Gardens®

Favorite
DESSERTS
MADE LIGHTER

BETTER HOMES AND GARDENS® BOOKS
Des Moines

BETTER HOMES AND GARDENS® BOOKS
An Imprint of Meredith® Books
President, Book Group: Joseph J. Ward
Vice President and Editorial Director: Elizabeth P. Rice
Executive Editor: Nancy N. Green
Managing Editor: Christopher Cavanaugh
Art Director: Ernest Shelton
Test Kitchen Director: Sharon Stilwell

FAVORITE DESSERTS MADE LIGHTER
Editor: Mary Major Williams
Writer: Patricia A. Ward
Recipe Development: Patricia A. Ward, Margaret M. Apice
Associate Art Director: Tom Wegner
Graphic Production Coordinator: Paula Forest
Production Manager: Doug Johnston
Test Kitchen Product Supervisor: Marilyn Cornelius
Food Stylist: Patricia A. Ward
Photographer: Maggie Wochele

On the cover: Black Forest Cake (page 106)

Meredith Corporation Corporate Officers:
Chairman of the Executive Committee: E. T. Meredith III
Chairman of the Board, President and Chief Executive Officer: Jack D. Rehm
Group Presidents: Joseph J. Ward, Books; William T. Kerr, Magazines; Philip A. Jones, Broadcasting; Allen L. Sabbag, Real Estate
Vice Presidents: Leo R. Armatis, Corporate Relations; Thomas G. Fisher, General Counsel and Secretary; Larry D. Hartsook, Finance; Michael A. Sell, Treasurer; Kathleen J. Zehr, Controller and Assistant Secretary

WE CARE!

All of us at Better Homes and Gardens® Books are dedicated to providing you with the information and ideas you need to create tasty foods.
We welcome your comments and suggestions. Write us at: Better Homes and Gardens® Books, Cookbook Editorial Department, RW-240, 1716 Locust St., Des Moines, IA 50309-3023

If you would like to order additional copies of any of our books, call 1-800-678-2803 or check with your local bookstore.

Our seal assures you that every recipe in *Favoite Desserts Made Lighter* has been tested in the Better Homes and Gardens® Test Kitchen. This means that each recipe is practical and reliable, and meets our high standards of taste appeal. We guarantee your satisfaction with this book for as long as you own it.

CONTENTS

Now you can enjoy the pleasures of dessert without the pangs of guilt. For this collection, we have created more than 150 tempting desserts by updating classic recipes, improving long-time favorites, and inventing brand new sweet treats. Many of our desserts have been lightened so they are lower in fat, cholesterol, calories, and/or sodium. Some were already light desserts. For the others, we compared the lightened desserts with recipes that were similar, but not lightened. Look for the percentages of fewer calories, less fat, cholesterol and/or sodium listed above the nutrition facts panel. This gives you an idea of how the recipes are lighter. (Ingredients were scrutinized and modified and sometimes the serving portions were adjusted to result in lighter recipes.) About 90 percent of these guilt-free creations have 250 calories or fewer per serving.

એ

On these pages, you'll find an array of luscious desserts featuring classic cream puffs, rich-tasting cheesecakes, fruit crisps, tender cakes, chewy cookies, flaky pastries, refreshing sorbets, and fresh fruit combinations.

એ

We also tell you how to lighten up your own family recipes with some creative substitutions. Sensible options for trimming fat and calories from almost any dessert are listed in the chart on page 6.

એ

Flip through the pages and the enticing photographs will show you that lightened desserts look luscious, too. For mouth-watering results every time, add an orange peel bow, fresh mint leaves, or an edible flower to one of these tantalizing treats. The section, *Sauces, Toppings, and Finishing Touches,* offers many easy-to-do presentation ideas.

એ

Favorite Desserts Made Lighter will help educate your palate, and before you know it, you'll prefer desserts made with less sugar and fat. Now you can end every meal on a sweet note and still maintain your healthy diet.

CUTTING THE FAT FOR A HEALTHY LIFESTYLE

There are two reasons for cutting fat and cholesterol from your daily diet:

1. Eating a high-fat diet is a threat to your health. When people eat too much fat, they are less likely to eat enough grains, fruits, and vegetables.

2. High-fat diets are related to heart disease, some kinds of cancers, and obesity. Nutrition studies show that high-fat diets, particularly those high in saturated fats, lead to increased cholesterol levels. Our editors and test kitchen staff have tried to find creative ways to reduce fat calories without sacrificing flavor.

FAT AND CHOLESTEROL FORMULA

Keep in mind three numbers—30, 10, and 300—they'll help you follow low-fat diet guidelines recommended for adult Americans:

• Keep fat intake to no more than 30 percent of the total calories in your diet over one or several days.

• To find out how many grams of fat you should have in your diet, figure the total number of calories you eat every day. Take 30 percent of your total calories and divide by 9. (There are 9 calories in every gram of fat.) For example, if your daily caloric consumption is 2,000 calories x .30 = 600 ÷ 9 = 67 grams of fat.

• To learn the amount of fat in foods, read the labels on the foods you buy and use the nutrition information on the recipes you make. The number of grams of fat provided can help you balance your own daily intake of fat.

• The amount of saturated fat in your diet should be kept to 10 percent of your total calories. For a 2,000 calorie diet, it would be about 22 grams. (2,000 calories x .10 = 200 ÷ 9 = 22 grams)

• Limit your cholesterol intake to 300 milligrams a day. Again check food labels and nutrition analyses on recipes you use. Remember that cholesterol is found only in foods of animal origin.

CREATIVE INGREDIENT SUBSTITUTIONS

Here are some general guidelines for reducing fat, saturated fat, and cholesterol when making desserts:

1. Use egg whites or a frozen egg product in place of whole eggs.
2. Nonstick cooking sprays are good substitutes for traditional fats. Now they come in several flavors—butter, olive oil, as well as unflavored—so you can choose the one that suits your family's taste.
3. Look for the lower-fat dairy products to replace cream cheese, sour cream, and whipped cream in your baked goods.
4. Add nonfat yogurt, applesauce, pureed fruits, and fruit juice to replace the fat cut from recipes.
5. Be aware that some nonfat foods are naturally higher in sodium than their lower-fat or regular-fat counterparts.

SIMPLE WAYS TO LIGHTEN DESSERTS

Instead of:	Substitute:
1 ounce baking chocolate	3 tablespoons unsweetened cocoa powder, 2 teaspoons sugar, and 1 tablespoon water
Butter	Cut the amount in half or replace with some applesauce in baked goods
1 whole egg	¼ cup frozen egg substitute or 2 egg whites or ¼ cup refrigerated (or fresh) low-cholesterol eggs
Sour cream	Use plain nonfat yogurt, fat-free dairy sour cream, or light dairy sour cream
Whole milk	Skim milk or evaporated skim milk
Nuts, chopped	Reduce by half and toast before adding to recipe

MORE ABOUT THE RECIPES

There are many low-fat alternatives for whipped cream on the market today. Your family may prefer reduced-fat frozen whipped dessert topping or an envelope of whipped dessert topping mix. If you'd like to whip your own homemade topping, turn to the recipes for Whipped Topping and Whipped Milk Topping on page 9. Both turn out light, fluffy toppings for only 7 or 8 calories and less than 1 gram of fat per tablespoon.

Read labels carefully when choosing any of the low-fat and lower-fat products in the supermarket. All of the products are different in both calories and fat content.

When you want a sweet treat with very few calories, look for this symbol throughout the book. It denotes the recipes (except cookies and sauces) that are 150 calories or less.

Nutrition Information
For each recipe we calculated the amount of calories, total fat, saturated fat, cholesterol, sodium, carbohydrate, dietary fiber, and protein per serving. You can use this information to balance your daily food and nutrition intake.

How was nutrition information calculated?
1. When ingredient options appear in the recipe, we used the first ingredient choice for the recipe analysis.
2. We omitted optional ingredients from the nutrition analysis.
3. Numbers are rounded off to the nearest whole number. For instance, if a nutrient is 0.001 to 0.499, it becomes <1, and if it's 0.500 to 0.999, it's rounded to 1.

SAUCES, TOPPINGS, AND FINISHING TOUCHES

Desserts are special and the lightened ones in this book are no exception. Desserts should command attention and look tempting as well as taste delicious. To keep our reduced-fat desserts uncomplicated, but spectacular-looking, we used simple garnishes throughout. Fresh berries, a sprig or two of fresh mint, candied edible flowers, slivered orange or lemon peel, or a dollop of whipped topping add just the right touch without overwhelming the dessert.

If you'd like to embellish your dessert a bit more, serve it with one of the 10 dessert sauces on the following pages. A slice of plain angel cake is simply heavenly topped with sugared fresh summer berries and one of our whipped toppings (page 9). The whipped toppings are made with evaporated milk or with dry milk powder—each has only eight calories and less than one gram of fat. Or try the colorful fruit sauces with one of the homemade sorbets, ices, or granitas in the Frozen Dessert chapter. Any one of these sauces will add a colorful and refreshing burst of flavor to plain nonfat yogurt or a light homemade custard.

You can showcase your dessert even more and dazzle everyone with a splashy painted plate, just like those served in fine restaurants. Colorful sauces are swirled around cakes, cheesecakes, or even poached fruit. Start with one of our thick fruit-based sauces (choose from the sauces on pages 10 to 13 or use the Fruit Puree, right), then follow these tips for designer plates.
- Fix and chill the fruit sauces up to a week in advance.
- Use simple or white plates to show off your designs.

- Spoon the sauce on the plate or use a plastic squeeze bottle. Or, try a heavy-plastic self-locking plastic bag and snip off a small piece of the corner.
- If the sauce is too thin, stir in a little powdered sugar. If too thick, stir in some fruit juice or water.
- Using a squeeze bottle or bag, you can make the following patterns:

  Lines: Applying steady pressure, move your hands steadily over each plate. Make straight or curved lines, zigzags, spirals, triangles, or circles.

  Dots: Squeeze gently, with your hands over one spot, then release the pressure and lift the bottle up and away.

  Hearts: Squeeze drops of fruit sauce onto a pool of another sauce or onto a plate. Draw a knife through the centers.

  Marble: Spoon small drops of sauce onto a pool of another sauce. Draw a knife through in a swirling motion.

  Chevron Stripes: Squeeze the sauce in parallel lines onto a pool of another sauce. Draw a knife through the fruit sauce across the parallel lines at a right angle. Start from one direction for the first stroke, then bring the knife from the other direction for the second. Continue alternating, bringing the knife from the opposite direction for each stroke.

Fruit Puree: In a blender container or food processor bowl, combine raspberries or peeled kiwi fruit with a little sugar. Cover; blend or process just till smooth. (If blended too much, the kiwi sauce can turn muddy.) If you like, press through a fine sieve to remove seeds.

WHIPPED TOPPING

This light topping is a little softer and foamier than the one made with evaporated milk. It beats up into fluffy peaks and is best when served immediately.

¼ cup ice water
1 tablespoon lemon juice
½ teaspoon vanilla

⅓ cup nonfat dry milk powder
1 tablespoon sugar

In a small mixing bowl combine ice water, lemon juice, and vanilla. Stir in dry milk powder. Beat with an electric mixer on high speed for 3 to 4 minutes or till soft peaks form (tips curl). Add sugar and beat for 1 minute more. Serve immediately. Makes about 1¼ cups.

Per Tablespoon:

Calories	7
Total fat	<1 g
Saturated fat	<1 g
Cholesterol	<1 mg
Sodium	6 mg
Carbohydrate	1 g
Fiber	<1 g
Protein	<1 g

WHIPPED MILK TOPPING

A light, sweet topping that adds a rich touch to your favorite desserts for only 8 calories a tablespoon and less than one gram of fat. The lemon juice adds a fresh taste and helps the milk whip to stiff peaks.

½ cup evaporated milk or
    evaporated skim milk

2 teaspoons lemon juice
½ teaspoon vanilla
⅓ cup sifted powdered sugar

Pour evaporated milk into an 8x8x2- or 9x9x2-inch baking pan. Freeze milk for 20 to 30 minutes or till soft ice crystals form throughout milk. Pour milk into a chilled mixing bowl. Beat with an electric mixer on high speed for 2 to 3 minutes or till soft peaks form (tips curl).

❧

Add lemon juice and vanilla; whip to mix well. Fold in powdered sugar. Serve immediately. Makes 2½ cups.

Per Tablespoon:

Calories	8
Total fat	<1 g
Saturated fat	<1 g
Cholesterol	1 mg
Sodium	3 mg
Carbohydrate	1 g
Fiber	<1 g
Protein	<1 g

CHOCOLATE DESSERT SAUCE

A rich, hot fudge sauce that's delightful whether served over ice milk or with slices of cake. Brown sugar and a tablespoon of margarine round out the chocolate flavor.

Per Tablespoon:

Calories	27
Total fat	1 g
Saturated fat	<1 g
Cholesterol	0 mg
Sodium	9 mg
Carbohydrate	6 g
Fiber	<1 g
Protein	<1 g

½ cup packed brown sugar
⅓ cup unsweetened cocoa
   powder
1 teaspoon cornstarch

¾ cup water
1 tablespoon margarine
1 teaspoon vanilla

In a small saucepan combine brown sugar, cocoa powder, and cornstarch. Add water. Cook and stir over medium heat till sauce is thickened and bubbly. Cook and stir for 2 minutes more. Remove from heat; stir in margarine and vanilla. Cover and chill thoroughly before serving. Makes about 1¼ cups.

ORANGE SAUCE

A light and tangy sauce thick enough to spoon directly on a plate to use as an artist's palette for your featured dessert. Try it with cheesecake or spice cake.

Per Tablespoon:

Calories	22
Total fat	1 g
Saturated fat	<1 g
Cholesterol	0 g
Sodium	<1 g
Carbohydrate	5 g
Fiber	<1 g
Protein	<1 g

¼ cup sugar
4 teaspoons cornstarch

½ teaspoon finely shredded
   orange peel
1 cup orange juice

In a small saucepan stir together sugar and cornstarch. Stir in orange peel and orange juice. Cook and stir till mixture is thickened and bubbly. Cook and stir for 2 minutes more. Remove from heat. Cool slightly before serving. Makes about 1 cup.

LEMON SAUCE

A light and zesty sauce just right for a square of warm, spicy gingerbread or with a slice of delicate angel food cake.

¼ cup sugar
1 tablespoon cornstarch
1 cup water
1 tablespoon margarine

1 teaspoon finely shredded lemon peel
3 tablespoons lemon juice

Per Tablespoon:

Calories	21
Total fat	1 g
Saturated fat	<1 g
Cholesterol	0 mg
Sodium	9 mg
Carbohydrate	4 g
Fiber	<1 g
Protein	<1 g

In a small saucepan combine sugar and cornstarch. Add water. Cook and stir over medium heat till mixture is thickened and bubbly. Cook and stir 2 minutes more. Remove from heat. Stir in margarine, lemon peel, and lemon juice. Cover surface with plastic wrap and cool well. Makes about 1 cup.

APRICOT SAUCE

You can make this tangy fruit sauce in advance and store it covered for a week or two in your refrigerator.

1 8¾-ounce can unpeeled apricot halves in light syrup
2 tablespoons brown sugar
¼ teaspoon finely shredded lemon peel

1 tablespoon lemon juice
1½ teaspoons cornstarch
1½ inches stick cinnamon

Per Tablespoon:

Calories	17
Total fat	<1 g
Saturated fat	<1 g
Cholesterol	0 mg
Sodium	1 mg
Carbohydrate	5 g
Fiber	<1 g
Protein	<1 g

Place *undrained* apricots in a blender container or food processor bowl. Cover; blend or process till smooth. Pour pureed apricots into a small saucepan. Add brown sugar, lemon peel, lemon juice, cornstarch, and cinnamon. Cook and stir over medium heat till mixture is thickened and bubbly. Cook and stir 2 minutes more. Remove from heat and cool thoroughly. Remove stick cinnamon. Store any leftover sauce in a covered container in the refrigerator for up to 2 weeks. Makes about 1 cup.

CINNAMON BLUEBERRY SAUCE

For a change of pace, add ½ teaspoon finely shredded lemon peel instead of the cinnamon. Either way this sauce embellishes your dessert sponge cake or vanilla ice milk quite nicely.

Per Tablespoon:

Calories	*14*
Total fat	*<1 g*
Saturated fat	*0 g*
Cholesterol	*0 mg*
Sodium	*<1 mg*
Carbohydrate	*4 g*
Fiber	*<1 g*
Protein	*0 g*

2 cups fresh or frozen blueberries, thawed
¼ cup sugar
1 teaspoon cornstarch
¼ teaspoon ground cinnamon
1 tablespoon lemon juice

In a medium saucepan mash about *half* of the blueberries with a potato masher. Set remaining blueberries aside. Stir sugar, cornstarch, and cinnamon into mashed blueberries. Cook and stir over medium heat till slightly thickened and bubbly. Cook and stir 2 minutes more. Remove from heat. Stir in lemon juice and remaining blueberries. Cover surface with plastic wrap and cool without stirring. Makes 1½ cups.

RASPBERRY SAUCE

Simple yet sophisticated, this fat-free sauce adds color and a burst of berry flavor to most any dessert.

Per Tablespoon:

Calories	*25*
Total fat	*<1 g*
Saturated fat	*<1 g*
Cholesterol	*0 mg*
Sodium	*<1 mg*
Carbohydrate	*7 g*
Fiber	*<1 g*
Protein	*<1 g*

½ cup sugar
2 teaspoons cornstarch
1 cup fresh or frozen raspberries, thawed
½ cup cranberry juice cocktail
1 tablespoon raspberry vinegar

In a medium saucepan combine sugar and cornstarch. Stir in ¾ *cup* of the raspberries, cranberry juice, and raspberry vinegar. Cook and stir till thickened and bubbly. Cook and stir for 2 minutes longer. Remove from heat. Stir in the remaining raspberries. Cool thoroughly. Makes 1⅓ cups.

NUTMEG SAUCE

Ladle this home-style sauce over your favorite fruit crisp or bread pudding. Apple juice and margarine give it a rich flavor.

¼ cup sugar
1 tablespoon cornstarch
1 cup apple juice

2 tablespoons margarine
½ teaspoon vanilla
⅛ teaspoon ground nutmeg

In a medium saucepan combine sugar and cornstarch. Gradually stir in apple juice. Add margarine. Cook and stir over medium heat till mixture is thickened and bubbly. Cook and stir 2 minutes more. Remove from heat. Stir in vanilla and nutmeg. Serve warm. Makes about 1 cup.

Per Tablespoon:

Calories	34
Total fat	1 g
Saturated fat	<1 g
Cholesterol	0 mg
Sodium	17 mg
Carbohydrate	5 g
Fiber	<1 g
Protein	<1 g

CHERRY SAUCE

Originally developed to serve with our dazzling Cream Puff Heart (page 26), we found this sauce to be versatile enough to top frozen yogurt, ice milk, or your favorite dessert.

2 tablespoons sugar
1 tablespoon cornstarch
1 teaspoon finely shredded
   orange peel

½ cup low-calorie cranberry juice
   cocktail or water
2 cups frozen pitted tart red
   cherries

In a medium saucepan combine sugar, cornstarch, and orange peel. Stir in the cranberry juice cocktail or water. Add the cherries. Cook and stir over medium heat till thickened and bubbly. Cook and stir for 2 minutes more. Remove from heat. Cool completely. Makes 1½ cups.

Per Tablespoon:

Calories	12
Total fat	<1 g
Saturated fat	<1 g
Cholesterol	0 mg
Sodium	1 mg
Carbohydrate	3 g
Fiber	<1 g
Protein	<1 g

FABULOUS DESSERTS

*F*or desserts that are spectacular to
present and easy on your diet, look no
further. Try the slimmed down Yogurt
Cheesecake with 260 calories per slice and
only 2 grams of saturated fat. Other
fat-trimmed cheesecakes include a creamy
Lime Cheesecake, fruit-topped mini
cheesecakes, or the more traditional
Cinnamon Ricotta Cheesecake. We've
lightened other classics for you,
too, including a selection of cream puff
recipes, flaky apple strudel, a creamy
chocolate-filled meringue, and a
super-light Strawberry Soufflé topped
with candied violets.

YOGURT CHEESECAKE

A combination of "Yogurt Cheese" and reduced-fat cream cheese produces a full-flavored cheesecake substantially lower in fat than traditional cheesecake.

40% fewer calories

80% less fat

90% less cholesterol

40% less sodium

1 cup crushed graham crackers
3 tablespoons sugar
2 tablespoons all-purpose flour
3 tablespoons margarine, melted
  Yogurt Cheese (see recipe
    page 32)
3 ounces reduced-fat cream
    cheese (Neufchâtel), softened

¾ cup sugar
2 tablespoons all-purpose flour
1½ teaspoons lemon juice
1 teaspoon vanilla
3 egg whites
¼ cup low-sugar orange
    marmalade spread
1 cup sliced fresh strawberries

Per Serving:

Calories	241
Total fat	6 g
Saturated fat	2 g
Cholesterol	8 mg
Sodium	207 mg
Carbohydrate	38 g
Fiber	<1 g
Protein	8 g

For crust, stir together crushed graham crackers, 3 tablespoons sugar, 2 tablespoons flour, and margarine. Press crumb mixture onto the bottom and 1 inch up the sides of an 8-inch springform pan. Bake in a 350° oven for 8 minutes. Cool on a wire rack.

ॐ

For filling, in a large mixing bowl combine Yogurt Cheese, cream cheese, the ¾ cup sugar, 2 tablespoons flour, lemon juice, and vanilla. Beat with an electric mixer on medium speed till smooth. Add egg whites and beat at low speed just till combined. Pour into crust. Bake in a 350° oven for 35 to 40 minutes or till cheesecake spreads evenly over entire surface when lightly shaken. Cool in pan on a wire rack. Cover and chill for several hours.

ॐ

To serve, in a small saucepan melt marmalade over low heat. Remove from heat; stir in strawberries. Let stand 10 minutes. Serve with cheesecake. Makes 10 servings.

LIME CHEESECAKE

For the photo, we spread the ½ cup sour cream topping on the chilled cheesecake. If you prefer a smooth topping, just spread it on the hot cheesecake as the recipe specifies.

Per Serving:

Calories	310
Total fat	19 g
Saturated fat	9 g
Cholesterol	53 mg
Sodium	335 mg
Carbohydrate	26 g
Fiber	<1 g
Protein	9 g

Nonstick spray coating
1 tablespoon crushed graham crackers
¾ cup crushed graham crackers
4 teaspoons all-purpose flour
1 tablespoon sugar
3 tablespoons margarine, melted
3 8-ounce packages reduced-fat cream cheese (Neufchâtel), softened
¾ cup sugar
1 8-ounce container light dairy sour cream
¼ cup all-purpose flour
¾ cup frozen egg product, thawed
½ cup skim milk
2 teaspoons finely shredded lime peel
¼ cup lime juice
1 teaspoon vanilla
10 drops green food coloring (optional)
½ cup light dairy sour cream
Lime slices (optional)
Lemon peel twists (optional)
Fresh mint (optional)

Spray a 9-inch springform pan with nonstick coating. Sprinkle the sides of the pan with the 1 tablespoon crushed graham crackers. Set pan aside.
For crust, in a small mixing bowl stir together the ¾ cup crushed graham crackers, 4 teaspoons flour, 1 tablespoon sugar, and melted margarine. Press the mixture onto the bottom of the prepared pan. Bake in a 350° oven for 5 minutes.

Meanwhile, in a large mixing bowl combine the cream cheese and ¾ cup sugar. Beat with an electric mixer on medium to high speed till smooth. Add the 8 ounces sour cream, ¼ cup flour, egg product, milk, lime peel, lime juice, vanilla, and, if desired, food coloring. Beat on low speed just till combined. Pour onto the baked crust. Place the pan in a shallow baking pan.

Bake in 350° oven for 45 to 50 minutes or till center appears nearly set when gently shaken. Remove from oven. Spread top with the ½ cup sour cream, *or* spread top with sour cream just before serving. Cool in pan on a wire rack for 15 minutes. Cover and chill cheesecake for 4 to 24 hours. Garnish with lime slices, lemon peel twists, and mint, if desired. Makes 12 servings.

75% fewer calories

95% less fat

95% less cholesterol

INDIVIDUAL FRUITED CHEESECAKES
These tiny gems offer all the taste of cheesecake for only 1 gram of fat per serving.

Per Serving:
Calories	*107*
Total fat	*1 g*
Saturated fat	*<1 g*
Cholesterol	*8 mg*
Sodium	*260 mg*
Carbohydrate	*16 g*
Fiber	*<1 g*
Protein	*8 g*

Nonstick spray coating
⅓ cup crushed vanilla wafers
    (8 wafers)
12 ounces fat-free cream cheese
    product
½ cup sugar
1 tablespoon all-purpose flour

1 teaspoon vanilla
¼ cup frozen egg product,
    thawed
¾ cup sliced strawberries,
    raspberries, sliced kiwi fruit,
    blueberries, sliced plums,
    and/or orange sections

Spray 10 muffin cups with nonstick coating. Sprinkle the bottom and sides of *each* with about *1 teaspoon* crushed vanilla wafers. Set aside.

ॐ

In a medium mixing bowl beat cream cheese product with an electric mixer on medium speed till smooth. Add sugar, flour, and vanilla. Beat on medium speed till smooth. Add egg product and beat just till combined. Divide evenly among the muffin cups.

ॐ

Bake in a 325° oven for 18 to 20 minutes or till set. Cool in pan on a wire rack for 5 minutes. Cover and chill for 4 to 24 hours. Remove cheesecakes from muffin cups. Just before serving, top with fresh fruit. Serves 10.

PUMPKIN CHEESECAKE DESSERT SQUARES

These spicy squares combine two favorites—pumpkin and cheesecake—in one easy-to-make dessert. As a special bonus, this combination is lower in fat and calories than either pumpkin pie or a traditional cheesecake.

65% fewer calories

75% less fat

85% less cholesterol

60% less sodium

Per Serving:

Calories_____118
Total Fat_____5 g
  Saturated fat_____2 g
Cholesterol_____19 mg
Sodium_____98 mg
Carbohydrate_____15 g
Fiber_____1 g
Protein_____2 g

Nonstick spray coating
1   cup crushed graham crackers
3   tablespoons sugar
1   tablespoon all-purpose flour
¼   cup margarine, melted
1   cup canned pumpkin
½   of an 8-ounce package
     reduced-fat cream cheese
     (Neufchâtel), softened
½   cup sugar
⅓   cup skim milk
1   egg
1   tablespoon all-purpose flour
1½ teaspoons pumpkin pie spice*
1   teaspoon vanilla

Spray an 8x8x2-inch baking pan with nonstick coating; set pan aside.

❧

In a mixing bowl combine the crushed graham crackers, 3 tablespoons sugar, 1 tablespoon flour, and melted margarine. Press mixture onto bottom of prepared baking pan. Bake in a 350° oven for 8 minutes.

❧

Meanwhile, in a mixing bowl combine the pumpkin and the cream cheese. Beat with an electric mixer on medium speed till smooth. Add the ½ cup sugar, milk, egg, 1 tablespoon flour, pumpkin pie spice, and vanilla. Beat on low speed till combined. Pour over baked crust.

❧

Bake in the 350° oven for 30 to 35 minutes or till filling is set. Cool thoroughly in pan on wire rack. Cut into squares. Store any leftovers in refrigerator. Makes 16 servings.

❧

*__Note__: You can substitute ¾ teaspoon ground *cinnamon,* ¼ teaspoon ground *allspice,* ¼ teaspoon ground *ginger,* and ¼ teaspoon ground *nutmeg* for the pumpkin pie spice.

CINNAMON RICOTTA CHEESECAKE

Depending on the capacity of your food processor, you may want to process half of the ricotta cheese at a time.

¾ cup finely crushed vanilla wafers (18 wafers)

2 tablespoons margarine, melted

1 tablespoon all-purpose flour

½ teaspoon ground cinnamon

2 15-ounce containers nonfat ricotta cheese (about 3¾ cups)

1 8-ounce carton frozen egg product, thawed

½ cup sugar

2 tablespoons all-purpose flour

1 teaspoon finely shredded lemon peel

1 teaspoon vanilla
Ground cinnamon

Per Serving:	
Calories	284
Total Fat	13 g
Saturated fat	6 g
Cholesterol	38 mg
Sodium	230 mg
Carbohydrate	27 g
Fiber	< 1 g
Protein	15 g

For crust, in a small mixing bowl stir together the crushed vanilla wafers, margarine, 1 tablespoon flour, and ½ teaspoon cinnamon. Press the mixture onto the bottom of a 9-inch springform pan. Bake in a 350° oven for 5 minutes. Cool on a wire rack.

❧

Meanwhile, in a food processor bowl place the ricotta cheese. Cover and process till smooth. Place cheese in a large mixing bowl. Stir in the egg product, sugar, 2 tablespoons flour, lemon peel, and vanilla till well combined. Pour over the crust. Sprinkle lightly with additional cinnamon.

❧

Bake in a 350° oven for 45 to 50 minutes or till center appears nearly set when gently shaken. Cool on a wire rack for 15 minutes.

❧

Loosen cake from the sides of the pan. Cool 30 minutes more; remove sides of pan. Cover and chill till serving time. Makes 8 servings.

INDIVIDUAL SCHAUM SHELLS

Based on a Austrian classic, schaum torte, our light airy meringue shells have a crisp outside and a soft marshmallow center—the perfect base for berries and whipped topping.

Nonstick spray coating
3 egg whites
¼ teaspoon cream of tartar
¾ cup sugar
1 teaspoon vanilla
½ teaspoon vinegar
4 cups blueberries, strawberries, raspberries and/or blackberries

2 tablespoons sugar
2 teaspoons raspberry liqueur or orange juice
1 tablespoon finely shredded orange peel
6 tablespoons reduced-fat frozen whipped dessert topping, thawed

Per Serving:

Calories	185
Total fat	1 g
Saturated fat	<1 g
Cholesterol	<1 g
Sodium	31 mg
Carbohydrate	41 g
Fiber	5 g
Protein	2 g

Spray a large baking sheet with nonstick coating; set aside.

❧

Place egg whites in a medium mixing bowl and let stand at room temperature for 30 minutes. Add cream of tartar to egg whites. Beat egg white mixture with an electric mixer on medium to high speed till soft peaks form. Gradually add the ¾ cup sugar, about *2 tablespoons* at a time, beating well on high speed after each addition. (Total beating time: 7 minutes.) Add vanilla and vinegar, beating 2 minutes more or till very stiff glossy peaks form (tips stand straight).

❧

Spoon mixture into 6 mounds on prepared baking sheet. With back of a spoon, spread to 3½-inch circles, building up the sides. Bake in a 300° oven for 30 minutes. Turn off oven. Let shells dry in oven with door closed for at least 1 hour. Remove from baking sheet to wire racks. Cool completely on wire racks.

❧

Meanwhile, in large bowl combine berries, 2 tablespoons sugar, raspberry liqueur or orange juice, and orange peel. Toss gently to mix. To serve, spoon berry mixture into each shell. Top with whipped topping. Makes 6 servings.

CINNAMON CHOCOLATE MERINGUE

Here's a dessert lover's dream—intense chocolate flavor with only one gram of fat per serving.

Per Serving:

Calories	*176*
Total fat	*1 g*
Saturated fat	*1 g*
Cholesterol	*1 mg*
Sodium	*62 mg*
Carbohydrate	*35 g*
Fiber	*<1 g*
Protein	*4 g*

½ cup packed brown sugar
⅓ cup unsweetened cocoa
     powder
½ cup evaporated skim milk
¼ cup frozen egg product,
     thawed
1 tablespoon cornstarch

1 1.3 ounce envelope whipped
     dessert topping mix
½ cup skim milk
     Meringue Pie Shell
     Shaved semisweet chocolate
     (optional)
     Fresh mint (optional)

For filling, in a medium saucepan combine brown sugar, cocoa powder, evaporated skim milk, egg product, and cornstarch. Cook and stir over medium heat till mixture is thickened and bubbly. (Mixture will be very thick.) Cook and stir for 2 minutes more. Remove from heat. Cool to room temperature.

❧

In a small mixing bowl prepare whipped dessert topping mix according to package directions except use the skim milk. Stir a small amount of whipped topping into chocolate filling to lighten it. Then fold remaining chocolate mixture into whipped topping mixture. Spoon mixture into Meringue Pie Shell. Cover and chill at least 2 hours or till serving time. Garnish with chocolate shavings and mint, if desired. Makes 8 servings.

MERINGUE PIE SHELL: Draw an 8-inch circle on heavy brown paper. Place paper on baking sheet. In a mixing bowl combine *2 egg whites,* ¼ teaspoon *ground cinnamon*, and ⅛ teaspoon *cream of tartar*. Beat with an electric mixer on medium speed till soft peaks form (tips curl). Gradually add ½ cup *sugar*, 1 tablespoon at a time, beating on high speed about 4 minutes more or till mixture forms stiff, glossy peaks (tips stand straight) and sugar dissolves. Spread *1 cup* of the meringue over 8-inch circle on the paper. Spoon remaining meringue into a decorating bag fitted with a large star tip (about ½ inch opening). Pipe a shell border on edge of meringue circle about 1¼ inches high. The completed shell should be about 9½ inches in diameter (Or, spread all of the meringue over a 9½-inch circle building up the edge.) Bake in a 300° oven for 40 minutes. Turn off oven. Let dry in oven with closed door for 1 hour. Cool on a wire rack. Carefully remove paper from meringue shell. Place on serving plate.

CREAM PUFF HEART

Pretty-as-a-picture, this cream-filled pastry tastes as scrumptious as it looks. The filling uses whipped topping mix instead of whipped cream making it a healthier dessert choice.

Per Serving:

Calories	183
Total fat	7 g
Saturated fat	1 g
Cholesterol	64 mg
Sodium	97 mg
Carbohydrate	25 g
Fiber	1 g
Protein	5 g

Nonstick spray coating
1   cup water
¼   cup margarine
1   cup all-purpose flour
3   egg whites

2   eggs
Cream Filling
Cherry Sauce (see recipe,
    page 13)
1   tablespoon powdered sugar

Spray a baking sheet with nonstick coating. Fold a 9x8½-inch piece of paper in half lengthwise. Draw half of a heart on the paper with the lengthwise center of the heart on the fold. Cut out heart. Open paper to full heart. Place the paper heart on the baking sheet. Trace around the heart with your finger. Set baking sheet aside.

❧

In a medium saucepan combine the water and margarine. Bring to boiling. Add the flour all at once, stirring vigorously. Cook and stir till mixture forms a ball that does not separate. Remove from heat. Cool 10 minutes. Add egg whites and eggs, one at a time, beating with a wooden spoon after each addition till smooth. Drop batter by heaping tablespoons into 20 mounds with sides touching onto the heart outline on the baking sheet.

❧

Bake in a 400° oven 35 to 40 minutes or till golden. Cool. Carefully split and remove the cream puff top. Remove any soft dough from inside. Just before serving, fill cream puff with Cream Filling. Replace top. Sift powdered sugar over top. Serve with Cherry Sauce. Makes 10 servings.

CREAM FILLING: In a heavy medium saucepan combine ⅓ cup *sugar* and 2 tablespoons *cornstarch*. Gradually stir in 1½ cups *skim milk*. Cook and stir over medium heat till mixture is thickened and bubbly. Cook and stir for 2 minutes more. Remove from heat. Gradually stir about *1 cup* of the hot mixture into 1 beaten *egg*. Return all of the egg mixture to the saucepan. Bring to boiling; cook and stir for 2 minutes more. Remove from heat. Stir in 1 teaspoon *vanilla*. Pour into bowl. Cover surface with plastic wrap; cool to room temperature. Meanwhile, in small mixing bowl combine one 1.3-ounce envelope *whipped topping mix* and ½ cup cold *skim milk*. Prepare according to package directions. Fold whipped dessert topping into cooled egg mixture. Cover; chill till serving time. Makes 3 cups.

MINTY CHOCOLATE ÉCLAIRS

When filled with frozen yogurt, these éclairs are lower in calories and fat than traditional ones. Served with the chocolate mint sauce, you won't think anything is missing.

Nonstick spray coating
1 cup water
¼ cup margarine
1 cup all-purpose flour
3 egg whites

2 eggs
Chocolate Mint Sauce
1 pint vanilla or chocolate frozen yogurt, softened
Powdered sugar (optional)

Per Serving:

Calories	*183*
Total Fat	*5 g*
Saturated fat	*1 g*
Cholesterol	*36 mg*
Sodium	*106 mg*
Carbohydrate	*29 g*
Fiber	*< 1 g*
Protein	*6 g*

Spray a baking sheet with nonstick coating; set baking sheet aside.

In a medium saucepan combine the water and margarine. Bring to boiling. Add the flour all at once, stirring vigorously. Cook and stir till mixture forms a ball that does not separate. Remove from heat. Cool for 10 minutes. Add the egg whites and the whole eggs, one at a time, beating with a wooden spoon after each addition till smooth. Spoon batter into a decorating bag fitted with a number 10 or larger tip. Pipe batter into twelve 4x¾x1-inch strips, about 3 inches apart, onto the prepared baking sheet.

Bake in a 400° oven about 35 minutes or till golden and firm. Remove from baking sheet; cool on a wire rack.

Split the éclairs and remove any soft dough from inside. Fill each éclair with frozen yogurt. If desired, lightly sift powdered sugar over éclairs. Makes 12 servings.

CHOCOLATE MINT SAUCE: In a small saucepan combine ¾ cup *sugar*, ⅓ cup *unsweetened cocoa powder*, and 4 teaspoons *cornstarch*. Stir in ⅔ cup *evaporated skim milk*. Cook and stir over medium heat till sauce is thickened and bubbly. Cook and stir for 2 minutes more. Remove from heat. Stir in ½ teaspoon *peppermint extract*. Cool sauce slightly before serving. Makes 1 cup.

LIGHT AND LEMONY CREAM PUFFS

By substituting egg whites for some of the whole eggs and using whipped topping instead of whipped cream in the filling, we've reduced the fat by 30 percent and the cholesterol by about 75 percent.

30% less fat

75% less cholesterol

50% less sodium

Nonstick spray coating	3 egg whites
1 cup water	2 eggs
¼ cup margarine	Lemon Filling
1 cup all-purpose flour	Powdered sugar (optional)
1 teaspoon finely shredded	Fresh raspberries (optional)
lemon peel	Orange peel strips (optional)
	Fresh mint (optional)

Per Serving:

Calories	243
Total Fat	10 g
Saturated fat	1 g
Cholesterol	43 mg
Sodium	108 mg
Carbohydrate	39 g
Fiber	< 1 g
Protein	4 g

Spray a baking sheet with nonstick coating; set baking sheet aside.

In a medium saucepan combine the water and margarine. Bring to boiling. Add the flour and lemon peel all at once, stirring vigorously. Cook and stir till mixture forms a ball that does not separate. Remove from heat. Cool for 10 minutes. Add the egg whites and the eggs, one at a time, beating with a wooden spoon after each addition till smooth. Drop batter by heaping tablespoons, about 3 inches apart, onto prepared baking sheet, making 10 mounds.

Bake in a 400° oven for 35 minutes or till golden and firm. Remove from baking sheet; cool on a wire rack. Just before serving, split 6 of the cream puffs and remove any soft dough from inside. Fill with Lemon Filling. If desired, sift powdered sugar over tops and garnish with raspberries, orange peel strips, and fresh mint. (Freeze the remaining cream puffs for another use.) Makes 6 servings.

LEMON FILLING: In a heavy small saucepan combine ⅔ cup *sugar* and ¼ cup *cornstarch*. Gradually stir in 1 cup *water*. Cook and stir over medium heat till mixture is thickened and bubbly. Cook and stir for 2 minutes more. Remove from heat. Stir in 2 teaspoons *margarine* till it melts. Gradually stir in ½ teaspoon *finely shredded lemon peel* and ¼ cup *lemon juice*. Stir in a few drops of *yellow food coloring*, if desired. Pour filling into a bowl. Cover; cool to room temperature. Fold in 1 cup thawed, reduced-fat frozen whipped dessert topping. Cover; chill till serving time. Makes about 1⅔ cups.

SUMMERTIME FRUIT TRIFLE

A version of an English classic that's perfect for hot weather entertaining with its layers of sponge cake squares, soft creamy custard, and fresh fruit.

Per Serving:

Calories	186
Total Fat	4 g
Saturated fat	1 g
Cholesterol	65 mg
Sodium	65 mg
Carbohydrate	33 g
Fiber	2 g
Protein	5 g

Simply Delicious Citrus Sponge
  Cake (see recipe, page 90)
⅓ cup sugar
¼ cup all-purpose flour
1½ cups skim milk
¼ cup frozen egg product,
  thawed
1 tablespoon margarine
1 teaspoon finely shredded
  orange peel
½ cup orange juice

2 tablespoons cream sherry or
  orange juice
2 cups fresh or frozen peeled
  peach slices
2 cups sliced strawberries
½ cup fresh or frozen blueberries
1 cup reduced-fat frozen
  whipped dessert topping,
  thawed
  Sliced strawberries (optional)
  Blueberries (optional)
  Fresh mint (optional)

Prepare Simply Delicious Citrus Sponge Cake in an 8x8x2-inch baking pan; set aside. (Do not prepare filling for cake.)

❧

Meanwhile, for custard sauce, in a heavy medium saucepan combine sugar and flour. Stir in skim milk and egg product. Cook and stir over medium heat till mixture is thickened and bubbly. Cook and stir 1 minute more. Remove from heat. Stir in margarine, orange peel, and ½ cup orange juice. Cool thoroughly.

❧

To assemble trifle, cut cake into 1½-inch cubes. In a 2-quart glass bowl arrange *half* of cake cubes. Sprinkle cake with *1 tablespoon* of the sherry or orange juice. Top with *half* of the peaches, strawberries, and blueberries. Pour *half* of custard over fruit. Repeat layers. Pipe or spread dessert topping on top. Cover and chill till serving time. If desired, garnish with additional strawberries, blueberries, and mint. Makes 10 servings.

ORANGE LADYFINGER BAVARIAN

Vary the flavor in this quick and easy recipe by changing the flavor of the sugar-free gelatin.

Per Serving:

Calories	104
Total Fat	2 g
Saturated fat	1 g
Cholesterol	29 mg
Sodium	94 mg
Carbohydrate	18 g
Fiber	< 1 g
Protein	4 g

1   4-serving-size package sugar-free orange-flavored gelatin
½   cup boiling water
⅔   cup cold orange juice
2   8-ounce cartons vanilla low-fat yogurt

1   3-ounce package ladyfingers, split
Orange peel curls (optional)
Fresh mint leaves (optional)

In a small mixing bowl dissolve gelatin in the boiling water. Stir in the orange juice. Chill till slightly thickened (consistency of unbeaten egg whites). Add yogurt. Beat with an electric mixer on medium speed for 1 to 2 minutes or till light and slightly foamy. Set aside.

Cut ladyfingers in half crosswise. Cover bottom of an 8-inch springform pan with ladyfinger halves. Place remaining halves, cut ends down, around sides of pan. Wrap foil around the outside bottom of the pan in case the filling leaks through the pan. Spoon gelatin mixture into pan. Cover and chill for 4 hours or till firm.

To serve, remove sides from pan. Garnish with orange peel curls and fresh mint leaves, if desired. Cut into wedges. Makes 8 servings.

YOGURT CHEESE

Line a large strainer or colander with a double thickness of 100% cotton cheesecloth and place over a large bowl. Spoon one 32-ounce carton plain nonfat yogurt (without gelatin) into the strainer or colander. Cover and chill about 15 hours or overnight. Discard the liquid in the bowl (whey). Use the curd (Yogurt Cheese). Wrap Yogurt Cheese in plastic wrap and chill till needed. Makes about 2 cups.

LAYERED STRAWBERRY DESSERT

An elegant dessert that's easy to whip up ahead of time.

50% fewer calories

25% less fat

Nonstick spray coating
3 cups strawberries, sliced
1 8-ounce container fat-free cream cheese product
½ cup sifted powdered sugar
⅓ cup lemon nonfat yogurt
1 teaspoon finely shredded lemon peel

2 cups reduced-fat frozen whipped dessert topping, thawed
2 vanilla wafers or chocolate wafers, crushed

Per Serving:

Calories	*123*
Total fat	*5 g*
Saturated fat	*<1 g*
Cholesterol	*6 mg*
Sodium	*220 mg*
Carbohydrate	*19 g*
Fiber	*1 g*
Protein	*7 g*

In a 2-quart clear glass bowl layer *half* of the strawberries. Set aside.

In medium mixing bowl combine cream cheese product, powdered sugar, lemon yogurt, and lemon peel. Beat with an electric mixer on medium speed till light and fluffy. Carefully spread mixture over strawberries.

Arrange remaining sliced strawberries on top. Spread with whipped topping. Sprinkle cookie crumbs on top. Cover and chill at least 2 hours. Makes 8 servings.

USING EGGS SAFELY

When using eggs in desserts and other recipes, be on the safe side—only use clean, fresh eggs. If your recipe calls for separating the yolks and whites, don't pass the yolk between shell halves. Instead, use an egg separator so that if bacteria is present on the shell, it won't contaminate the yolk or white. Also, avoid getting any eggshell in with the raw eggs.

Eating uncooked or slightly cooked eggs in foods may be harmful because of possible bacterial contamination from salmonella. The individuals most susceptible include the elderly, infants, pregnant women, and those who are already ill. Check with your doctor to see if you are at risk. If you are, you probably should avoid eating foods that contain raw or partially cooked eggs. Healthy people should eat raw eggs with discretion.

CHILLED STRAWBERRY SOUFFLÉ

It's easy to candy your own fresh violets. Use pesticide-free violets and wash thoroughly. Let dry and brush surfaces with light corn syrup and then sprinkle with sugar. Let dry on wire racks.

Per Serving:

Calories	67
Total fat	<1 g
Saturated fat	<1 g
Cholesterol	<1 mg
Sodium	31 mg
Carbohydrate	14 g
Fiber	2 g
Protein	2 g

EXTRA-LIGHT

1 10-ounce package frozen strawberries, thawed	2 tablespoons sugar
½ cup water	1 1.3-ounce envelope whipped dessert topping mix
1 envelope unflavored gelatin	½ cup skim milk
1 tablespoon lemon juice	Candied violets (optional)
3 egg whites (see tip, page 33)	Lemon balm leaves (optional)

To make a collar for a 1-quart soufflé dish, cut a 24-inch length of foil. Fold lengthwise into thirds, making a 4-inch-wide strip. Place strip around outside of the soufflé dish so it extends 3 inches above the rim. Pull tight and secure with tape at the point the foil overlaps.

In a blender container or food processor bowl place strawberries and water. Cover and blend or process till smooth. Pour mixture into a heavy small saucepan. Stir in gelatin; let stand 5 minutes to soften. Cook and stir over low heat till gelatin is completely dissolved. Remove from heat. Stir in lemon juice. Transfer mixture to a large mixing bowl. Cover and chill for 30 to 60 minutes or till the mixture is the consistency of corn syrup, stirring occasionally.

Remove the gelatin mixture from the refrigerator (it will continue to set). In a medium mixing bowl immediately beat the egg whites with an electric mixer on medium speed till soft peaks form (tips curl). Gradually add sugar, about *1 tablespoon* at a time, beating on high speed till stiff peaks form (tips stand straight). When gelatin is partially set (consistency of unbeaten egg whites), fold into the egg white mixture.

In a chilled bowl beat whipped dessert topping mix according to package directions except use skim milk. Fold the whipped topping into the gelatin mixture. Spoon mixture into prepared souffle dish. Cover and chill for 6 hours or till set. If desired, garnish souffle with candied violets and lemon balm leaves. Makes 10 servings.

POPPY SEED DESSERT

If you chill the filling a while before spooning it into the pan, it will mound higher and look light and fluffy.

½ cup crushed graham crackers
¼ cup all-purpose flour
2 tablespoons finely chopped
    walnuts, toasted
2 tablespoons margarine, melted
⅔ cup sugar
1 envelope unflavored gelatin
2 tablespoons cornstarch
1 to 2 tablespoons poppy seeds

1¾ cups skim milk
1 teaspoon vanilla
5 egg whites (see tip, page 33)
½ teaspoon cream of tartar
⅓ cup sugar
   Raspberry Puree
   Fresh raspberries and/or
     blackberries (optional)
   Fresh mint (optional)

For crust, in a small mixing bowl combine the crushed graham crackers, flour, toasted walnuts, and melted margarine. Press the mixture onto the bottom of a 9-inch springform pan. Bake in a 325° oven about 12 minutes or till golden brown. Cool in pan on a wire rack.

In a heavy medium saucepan stir together the ⅔ cup sugar, gelatin, cornstarch, and poppy seeds. Stir in skim milk all at once. Cook and stir over medium heat till mixture is thickened and bubbly. Cook and stir 2 minutes more. Remove from heat. Stir in vanilla. Chill till mixture mounds, stirring occasionally to prevent lumps.

In a large mixing bowl combine egg whites and cream of tartar. Beat with an electric mixer on medium speed till soft peaks form (tips curl). Gradually add ⅓ cup sugar, *1 tablespoon* at a time, beating on medium speed till stiff peaks form (tips stand straight). Fold custard mixture into egg white mixture. Pour into pan over the crust. Cover; chill for 6 to 24 hours.

Serve with Raspberry Puree and, if desired, fresh raspberries, blackberries, and mint. Makes 12 servings.

RASPBERRY PUREE: In a blender container or food processor bowl place 1 cup fresh or thawed, frozen *raspberries* and 1 tablespoon *sugar.* Cover and blend or process till berries are pureed. Press berries through a fine-mesh sieve; discard seeds. Cover and chill till serving.

LEMON YOGURT CRÈME

To decorate this delightful dessert, look for small flowers that are safe to eat and were grown without pesticides. Grow your own or buy them in the supermarket.

60% less fat

¼ cup cold water
1½ teaspoons unflavored gelatin
1 Vanilla bean or 1 tablespoon vanilla
  Yogurt Cheese (see recipe, page 32)
1 cup sifted powdered sugar
1 teaspoon finely shredded lemon peel

Edible flowers such as violets, rose petals, and/or pansies (optional)
Assorted fresh fruits such as grapes, sliced pears, apple wedges, and/or kumquats (optional)
Lemon leaves (optional)

In a small saucepan combine cold water and gelatin; let stand for 5 minutes to soften. Heat and stir over low heat till gelatin is dissolved. Remove from heat. Set aside.

❧

Cut the vanilla bean (if using) in half. Split *one* of the halves with a sharp knife. Scrape out the powder-fine seeds; set seeds aside. Store the remaining half of vanilla bean in a tightly covered container in the refrigerator for up to 6 months.

❧

In a large mixing bowl stir together Yogurt Cheese, powdered sugar, lemon peel, the gelatin mixture, and the vanilla bean seeds or vanilla. Line one 2-cup heart-shaped mold or baking pan, or four ½-cup heart-shaped molds, ramekins or other molds with plastic wrap or 100% cotton cheesecloth, using enough so the wrap or cheesecloth hangs over sides of mold(s) or pan. If desired, place edible flowers, face down, in bottom(s) of the mold(s) or pan in a decorative pattern. Carefully spoon yogurt mixture over flowers. Smooth top(s) with a metal spatula. Cover surface with plastic wrap; chill for 4 hours or till set.

❧

To serve, place platter (or plates for the smaller molds) on top of the mold(s) or pan and invert. Carefully remove the mold(s) or pan. The flowers should be on top. Carefully remove the plastic wrap or cheesecloth. Serve with assorted fresh fruit and garnish with lemon leaves, if desired. Makes 4 servings.

RASPBERRY LEMON SQUARES

For a lovely lemon mousse, skip the graham cracker crust and the raspberry sauce. Spoon the chilled filling into eight graceful stemmed glasses, and garnish with fresh raspberries and lemon peel curls.

25% fewer calories

55% less fat

95% less cholesterol

40% less sodium

¾ cup crushed graham crackers
2 tablespoons sugar
3 tablespoons margarine, melted
½ cup sugar
¼ cup all-purpose flour
1 envelope unflavored gelatin
1¾ cups skim milk
1 teaspoon vanilla
1 teaspoon finely shredded
   lemon peel

3 egg whites (see tip, page 33)
¼ teaspoon cream of tartar
½ cup sugar
1½ cups reduced-fat frozen
   whipped dessert topping,
   thawed
Easy Raspberry Sauce
Fresh raspberries (optional)

Per Serving:

Calories	262
Total fat	7 g
Saturated fat	1 g
Cholesterol	1 mg
Sodium	136 mg
Carbohydrate	48 g
Fiber	3 g
Protein	5 g

For crust, in a small mixing bowl combine the crushed graham crackers, 2 tablespoons sugar, and melted margarine. Press the mixture onto the bottom of a 9x9x2-inch baking pan. Bake in a 375° oven for 5 minutes. Cool in pan on a wire rack.

❧

In a heavy medium saucepan stir together the ½ cup sugar, flour, and gelatin. Stir in the skim milk all at once. Cook and stir over medium heat till mixture is thickened and bubbly. Cook and stir 1 minute more. Remove from heat. Cool. Stir in the vanilla and lemon peel.

❧

In a medium mixing bowl combine the egg whites and cream of tartar. Beat with an electric mixer on medium speed till soft peaks form (tips curl). Add ½ cup sugar, *1 tablespoon* at a time, beating on medium speed till stiff peaks form (tips stand straight). Fold egg whites and whipped topping into cooled gelatin mixture. Pour over crust in pan. Cover and chill, about 2 hours or till set.

❧

To serve, cut into squares. Top with Easy Raspberry Sauce and, if desired, fresh raspberries. Makes 9 servings.

EASY RASPBERRY SAUCE: In a medium saucepan, combine one 12-ounce package frozen loose-pack *raspberries*, ½ cup *water*, ¼ cup *sugar*, and 4 teaspoons *cornstarch*. Cook and stir over medium heat till mixture is bubbly. Cook and stir 2 minutes more. Remove from the heat. Cool slightly. Strain sauce through a sieve to remove seeds. Cool thoroughly. Makes 1 cup.

GOLDEN APPLE STRUDEL

For ease in working with frozen phyllo dough, it's best to thaw it at least 8 hours or overnight to prevent damp spots that could cause the sheets to stick together.

Per Serving:

Calories	119
Total Fat	5 g
Saturated fat	1 g
Cholesterol	0 mg
Sodium	109 mg
Carbohydrate	19 g
Fiber	1 g
Protein	2 g

Nonstick spray coating
2 medium apples, peeled, cored and thinly sliced (2 cups)
1 tablespoon light raisins
1 tablespoon brown sugar
¼ teaspoon ground cinnamon
⅛ teaspoon ground nutmeg
6 sheets frozen phyllo dough (17x12-inch rectangles), thawed
3 tablespoons margarine, melted
2 teaspoons powdered sugar

Spray a 15x10x1-inch baking pan with nonstick coating; set aside.

❧

In a medium mixing bowl combine apples, raisins, brown sugar, cinnamon, and nutmeg. Toss to mix. Set aside.

❧

Place two sheets of phyllo on waxed paper. Brush with some of the melted margarine. Repeat two more times with the remaining phyllo and margarine. Place the apples in a 2-inch-wide strip along one long edge of phyllo, leaving 1½ inches at short sides. Fold in along short sides. Roll up tightly, beginning from long side with apples. Place roll, seam-side down, in prepared pan. Brush roll with any remaining margarine.

❧

Bake in a 350° oven for 30 to 35 minutes or till golden. Cool slightly; loosen strudel from pan. Cool in pan on a wire rack. Sift powdered sugar over strudel. Makes 8 servings.

PEACH-FILLED PHYLLO BUNDLES

Frozen unsweetened peaches can be used here instead of the fresh ones. After thawing, be sure to blot them with paper towels before combining with the other ingredients.

70% fewer calories

90% less fat

no cholesterol

50% less sodium

3 medium peaches, peeled, pitted and coarsely chopped, or 2¼ cups frozen unsweetened peach slices, thawed and coarsely chopped
2 tablespoons sugar
1 tablespoon finely chopped crystallized ginger

1 tablespoon all-purpose flour
1 teaspoon lemon juice
   Butter-flavored nonstick spray coating
4 sheets frozen phyllo dough (17x12-inch rectangles), thawed
2 teaspoons powdered sugar

Per Serving:

Calories	148
Total Fat	2 g
Saturated fat	< 1 g
Cholesterol	0 mg
Sodium	77 mg
Carbohydrate	32 g
Fiber	1 g
Protein	3 g

For filling, in a medium mixing bowl, combine peaches, sugar, ginger, flour, and lemon juice. Toss to mix; set aside.

❧

Spray four 6-ounce custard cups with nonstick coating. Set aside. Spray one phyllo sheet with nonstick coating. Place another sheet of phyllo on top of the first sheet, then spray with nonstick coating. Repeat twice. Cut stack lengthwise and then crosswise to form 4 rectangles. Using 1 stack of phyllo, gently ease center of phyllo into bottom and up side of one custard cup (phyllo will hang over). Spoon a heaping *½ cup* of the peach filling into center. Bring phyllo up over filling, pinching together to form a ruffled edge. Spray again with nonstick coating. Repeat with remaining phyllo and filling. Place in a 15x10x1-inch shallow baking pan.

❧

Bake in a 375° oven for 20 minutes. Cool slightly. Sift powdered sugar over pastry tops before serving. Makes 4 servings.

MINIATURE CANNOLI CONES

Traditional Italian cannoli shells are deep-fried before filling. For this recipe, we substituted a crisp cookie that's shaped into cones and filled with a nonfat ricotta cheese filling.

75% fewer calories

75% less fat

65% less sodium

Nonstick spray coating
2   egg whites
⅓   cup all-purpose flour
⅓   cup sugar
2   tablespoons margarine, melted
½   teaspoon vanilla
½   cup nonfat ricotta cheese
1   tablespoon sugar

½   teaspoon finely shredded
      orange peel
⅛   teaspoon ground cinnamon
¾   cup reduced-fat frozen
      whipped dessert topping,
      thawed
1   tablespoon miniature
      semisweet chocolate pieces

Per Cookie:

Calories	*57*
Total fat	*2 g*
Saturated fat	*<1 g*
Cholesterol	*1 mg*
Sodium	*30 mg*
Carbohydrate	*8 g*
Fiber	*<1 g*
Protein	*2 g*

Spray a cookie sheet with nonstick coating; set aside.

In a medium mixing bowl combine egg whites, flour, ⅓ cup sugar, melted margarine, and vanilla. Stir till smooth. Drop batter by teaspoonfuls, about 4 inches apart, on prepared cookie sheet. Spread each to make 3½-inch circles. (Bake 3 or 4 cookies at a time.)

Bake in a 375° oven about 6 minutes or till bottoms of cookies are lightly browned. Immediately loosen cookies from cookie sheet. Turn over and roll up each to form a cone. (*Or*, wrap around metal cannoli cones; remove cookies from cones while still warm.) Cool on a wire rack, seam side down. (If cookies become too stiff to roll, return briefly to oven to soften.) Repeat with remaining batter.

For cheese filling, in a small mixing bowl stir together ricotta cheese, 1 tablespoon sugar, orange peel, and cinnamon. Fold in whipped dessert topping and chocolate chips. Cover and chill till serving time.

To serve, pipe or spoon cheese filling into cookie cones. Serve immediately. Makes 16.

HOT CHOCOLATE SOUFFLÉ

This soufflé proves that heart-healthy desserts can be as appealing as higher-fat ones. We've cut both fat and cholesterol by using evaporated skim milk and eliminating egg yolks.

30% fewer calories

90% less fat

95% less cholesterol

Nonstick spray coating
¼ cup unsweetened cocoa
    powder
¼ cup sugar
2 tablespoons cornstarch
1 cup evaporated skim milk
½ cup frozen egg product,
    thawed

1 tablespoon rum or ½ teaspoon
    rum flavoring
4 egg whites
½ teaspoon cream of tartar
¼ cup sugar
    Powdered sugar
    Whipped Topping or Whipped
      Milk Topping (see recipes,
      page 9)

Per Serving:

Calories	145
Total fat	1 g
Saturated fat	<1 g
Cholesterol	1 mg
Sodium	113 mg
Carbohydrate	25 g
Fiber	<1 g
Protein	8 g

To make a collar for a 1-quart soufflé dish, cut a 24-inch length of foil. Fold lengthwise into thirds, making a 4-inch-wide strip. Spray one side of strip with nonstick coating. Place strip, coated side in, around the outside of the soufflé dish so it extends about 2 inches above the rim. Pull tight and secure with tape at the point the foil overlaps.

In a medium saucepan combine cocoa powder, ¼ cup sugar, and cornstarch. Add evaporated skim milk all at once. Cook and stir over medium heat till mixture is thickened and bubbly. Cook and stir 2 minutes more. Stir some of the cocoa mixture into the egg product. Then return all of the egg product mixture to the saucepan. Bring to a gentle boil. Remove from heat. Stir in rum or rum flavoring.

In a large mixing bowl beat the egg whites and cream of tartar with an electric mixer on medium speed till soft peaks form (tips curl). Add ¼ cup sugar, *1 tablespoon* at a time, beating on high speed till stiff peaks form (tips stand straight). Fold a small amount of beaten egg white mixture into chocolate mixture to lighten it. Then fold chocolate mixture into remaining beaten egg whites. Turn mixture into prepared soufflé dish.

Bake in a 350° oven for 35 to 40 minutes or till a knife inserted near the center comes out clean. Remove the collar; sift powdered sugar over top. Serve immediately with Whipped Topping or Whipped Milk Topping. Makes 6 servings.

ORANGE-BANANA CREPES

For best results when making crepes, use a nonstick skillet or one that's been specially seasoned so the crepes don't stick. It's a good idea to keep one skillet just for crepe-making.

Per Serving:

Calories	237
Total Fat	6 g
Saturated fat	1 g
Cholesterol	1 mg
Sodium	107 mg
Carbohydrate	43 g
Fiber	1 g
Protein	5 g

⅔	cup skim milk
½	cup all-purpose flour
1	egg white
1	tablespoon sugar
	Nonstick spray coating

1	large banana
1	orange, peeled and sectioned
2	tablespoons margarine
½	cup orange juice
¼	cup packed brown sugar

For crepe batter, in a small mixing bowl combine the milk, flour, egg white, and granulated sugar. Beat with a rotary beater till well mixed. Spray a 6-inch skillet with nonstick coating, then heat the skillet over medium heat. Remove from heat. For each crepe, spoon *2 tablespoons* of the batter into hot skillet. Lift and tilt the skillet to spread batter. Return to the heat; brown crepe on one side only. (Or, cook on an inverted crepe maker according to manufacturer's directions.) Invert the pan over paper towels; remove the crepe. Repeat with the remaining batter to make 8 crepes. Lightly spray skillet occasionally with nonstick coating, allowing skillet to cool slightly between crepes.

Cut the banana in half crosswise. Cut each half into quarters lengthwise. You should have 8 pieces. Place a piece of banana and one or two orange sections on each crepe. Fold opposite sides of crepes over fruit.

For sauce, in a large skillet melt margarine. Add orange juice and brown sugar. Cook and stir till mixture bubbles; reduce heat and simmer about 4 minutes or till mixture is slightly thickened. Add filled crepes to skillet. Heat through, spooning sauce over crepes. Makes 4 servings.

ORANGE SKILLET SOUFFLÉ

Impress dinner guests with this spectacular dessert, served straight from the oven with a dusting of powdered sugar.

45% fewer calories

80% less fat

60% less cholesterol

40% less sodium

Nonstick spray coating
1 cup orange juice
½ cup nonfat dry milk powder
2 tablespoons granulated sugar
2 tablespoons cornstarch
2 egg yolks

1 teaspoon finely shredded orange peel
6 egg whites
½ teaspoon cream of tartar
¼ cup granulated sugar
Powdered sugar

Per Serving:

Calories	103
Total fat	2 g
Saturated fat	<1 g
Cholesterol	54 mg
Sodium	67 mg
Carbohydrate	17 g
Fiber	<1 g
Protein	5 g

Spray a 10-inch oven-going* skillet or a 2-quart rectangular baking dish with nonstick coating; set aside. Separate egg yolks into medium bowl; set aside.

In a small saucepan combine orange juice, dry milk powder, 2 tablespoons granulated sugar, and cornstarch. Cook and stir over medium heat till mixture is thickened and bubbly. (Mixture may appear curdled before it boils.) Cook and stir 2 minutes more. Stir about *half* of the hot mixture into the egg yolks. Then return all of the egg yolk mixture to the saucepan. Cook and stir 2 minutes more. Stir in orange peel. Remove from heat; set aside.

In a large mixing bowl beat egg whites and cream of tartar with an electric mixer on high speed till soft peaks form (tips curl). Gradually add ¼ cup granulated sugar, *1 tablespoon* at a time, beating till stiff peaks form (tips stand straight). Stir about *1 cup* of the egg white mixture into yolk mixture to lighten. Then gently fold yolk mixture into remaining egg white mixture. Spoon mixture into prepared skillet or baking dish.

Bake in a 375° oven for 25 to 30 minutes or till puffed and golden. Sift powdered sugar over top. Serve immediately. Makes 8 to 10 servings.

*To make skillet oven-going, cover handle with aluminum foil.

HOME-STYLE DESSERTS

*I*n this section you will find your favorite desserts, updated for today's tastes and better health. You won't miss the fat, cholesterol, and calories in these winning desserts that remind you of grandmother's cooking. There's a light bread pudding served with a nutmeg sauce, an easy-to-make Summertime Berry Shortcake, several rice puddings, and a baked custard. For something a bit different, try our dessert pizza, a thin, fudgy brownie crust with a topping of sliced fresh fruits, and drizzled with chocolate sauce.

LEMON PUDDING CAKE

Look for a creamy pudding layer topped with a light lemon sponge in this easy baked dessert.
To update the traditional recipe we added a little more flour and reduced the egg yolks.

50% fewer calories

70% less fat

65% less cholesterol

4   egg whites
2   egg yolks
2   teaspoons finely shredded
      lemon peel
⅓   cup lemon juice
1   tablespoon margarine, melted

⅔   cup sugar
⅓   cup all-purpose flour
¼   teaspoon salt
1½ cups skim milk
      Vanilla frozen yogurt or ice
        milk (optional)

Per Serving:

Calories	121
Total fat	3 g
Saturated fat	1 g
Cholesterol	48 mg
Sodium	128 mg
Carbohydrate	21 g
Fiber	<1 g
Protein	4 g

In a medium mixing bowl place egg whites. Let stand at room temperature for 30 minutes. Beat with an electric mixer on high speed till soft peaks form (tips curl). Set beaten egg whites aside.

In a large mixing bowl combine egg yolks, lemon peel, lemon juice, and melted margarine. Beat with an electric mixer on high speed till well mixed. In another mixing bowl combine sugar, flour, and salt. Using electric mixer on low speed, add sugar mixture to egg yolk mixture alternately with skim milk, beating just till combined after each addition. Fold about one-third of the flour mixture into the egg whites. Then fold egg white mixture into the remaining flour mixture. Pour into a 2-quart square baking dish. Place baking dish in a large baking pan; pour hot water into baking pan around baking dish to a depth of 1 inch.

Bake in a 350° oven about 40 minutes or till top is golden brown.

Remove large pan from oven. Carefully lift the baking dish from water; transfer to a wire rack. Serve warm. Top with frozen yogurt or ice milk, if desired. Makes 9 servings.

MIXED FRUIT CLAFOUTI

Clafouti is a fruit and custardlike dessert that hails from the French countryside.
This version substitutes frozen egg product for whole eggs and skim milk for whole milk.

Per Serving:

Calories	210
Total fat	6 g
Saturated fat	1 g
Cholesterol	1 mg
Sodium	48 mg
Carbohydrate	36 g
Fiber	2 g
Protein	5 g

Nonstick spray coating
1   cup skim milk
¾   cup all-purpose flour
½   cup frozen egg product, thawed
¼   cup sugar
2   tablespoons cooking oil
1   teaspoon vanilla
¼   teaspoon almond extract

2   medium plums, pitted and sliced
2   medium peeled peaches or nectarines, pitted and sliced
1   cup sweet cherries, halved and pitted
1   tablespoon powdered sugar

Spray a 9-inch pie plate or six 5-inch quiche dishes or six 10-ounce custard cups with nonstick coating; set aside.

❧

In a small mixing bowl combine skim milk, flour, egg product, sugar, cooking oil, vanilla, and almond extract. Using an electric mixer on low speed or a rotary beater beat till smooth. Arrange plums, peaches or nectarines, and cherries in prepared pie plate, quiche dishes, or custard cups. Pour batter over fruit.

❧

Bake in a 375° oven for 25 to 30 minutes or till puffy and lightly browned. Sift powdered sugar over top. Serve warm. Makes 6 servings.

SPICED PUMPKIN FLANS

These individual baked custards are enriched with pumpkin puree and a topping of caramelized sugar.

1 cup canned or pureed cooked pumpkin or butternut squash	¼ teaspoon ground ginger
2 egg whites	⅛ teaspoon ground cloves
1 egg	½ cup sugar
¼ cup sugar	1 12-ounce can evaporated skim milk
¾ teaspoon ground cinnamon	

In medium bowl combine pumpkin or squash, egg whites, egg, the ¼ cup sugar, cinnamon, ginger, and cloves. Beat with a wire whisk or rotary beater till smooth; set aside.

❧

Place the ½ cup sugar in a heavy small skillet. Cook over medium-high heat till sugar begins to melt, shaking skillet occasionally to heat sugar evenly. Do not stir. Reduce heat to low; cook about 5 minutes more or till sugar is melted and golden. Stir as necessary after sugar begins to melt and as mixture bubbles. Remove from heat; quickly spoon the syrup into six 6-ounce custard cups; set aside.

❧

In small saucepan over medium heat, cook and stir evaporated skim milk till very hot but not boiling. Remove from heat.

❧

Slowly stir hot milk into pumpkin mixture. Pour into prepared custard cups. Place cups in a large baking pan. Pour hot water into baking pan around custard cups filling to a depth of 1 inch.

❧

Bake in a 325° oven for 30 to 35 minutes or till a knife inserted halfway between center and edge comes out clean. Remove cups from water. Cool in cups on a wire rack. Cover and chill at least 2 hours. To serve, unmold onto dessert plates. Makes 6 servings.

ORANGE-RICE CUSTARD

A hint of orange peel adds a calorie-free flavor boost to this reduced-fat, lower cholesterol style of rice pudding.

Per Serving:

Calories	132
Total fat	1 g
Saturated fat	<1 g
Cholesterol	1 mg
Sodium	91 mg
Carbohydrate	25 g
Fiber	<1 g
Protein	5 g

1½ cups skim milk
1 teaspoon finely shredded orange peel
⅔ cup long grain rice
1 tablespoon sugar
1 8-ounce carton frozen egg product, thawed

¾ cup sugar
1 tablespoon margarine, melted
2 cups skim milk
Nonstick spray coating
Thin strips of orange peel (optional)
Fresh mint sprigs (optional)

In a medium saucepan combine 1½ cups skim milk, finely shredded orange peel, rice, and the 1 tablespoon sugar. Bring to boiling. Reduce heat. Cover and simmer for 15 to 20 minutes or till liquid is absorbed and rice is tender. Remove from heat.

❧

In a large mixing bowl combine egg product, the ¾ cup sugar, margarine, and 2 cups skim milk. Mix till sugar is dissolved. Stir in rice mixture.

❧

Spray a 2-quart square baking dish with nonstick coating. Transfer rice mixture to dish. Spread evenly in dish. Place dish in a large baking pan; pour hot water into baking pan around baking dish to a depth of 1 inch.

❧

Bake in a 350° oven for 35 minutes. Stir rice mixture. Bake for 10 to 15 minutes more or till firm around edges and almost set in center. Remove large pan from oven. Carefully lift baking dish from water; transfer to a wire rack. Cool slightly. Serve warm or chilled. To serve warm, spoon custard into dessert dishes. To serve chilled, cut custard into squares. Garnish with orange peel strips and mint, if desired. Makes 10 servings.

BAKED MAPLE CUSTARDS

So easy to bake, these delicately flavored custards make great weekday desserts.

45% fewer calories

65% less fat

65% less cholesterol

3 tablespoons maple-flavored
   syrup
2 eggs
2 egg whites

2 cups skim milk
¼ cup sugar
1 teaspoon vanilla

Per Serving:

Calories_____119
Total Fat_____2 g
  Saturated fat_____1 g
Cholesterol_____72 mg
Sodium_____92 mg
Carbohydrate_____20 g
Fiber_____0 g
Protein_____6 g

Divide maple-flavored syrup among six 6-ounce custard cups; set cups aside.

❧

In medium mixing bowl combine eggs, egg whites, milk, sugar, and vanilla. Beat till well combined but not foamy. Place prepared custard cups in a 13x9x2-inch baking pan. Pour egg mixture into custard cups. Pour boiling water into baking pan around custard cups to a depth of 1 inch.

❧

Bake in a 325° oven for 35 to 40 minutes or till a knife inserted near the centers comes out clean. Carefully lift custard cups from water. Transfer to a wire rack. Serve warm or cool completely and chill. To unmold, loosen edges of custards with a spatula, slipping point of spatula down sides to let air in; invert onto dessert plates. Makes 6 servings.

APPLE CRANBERRY CRISP

This colorful crisp blends the tartness of apples with sweet pungent cranberries. When served with nonfat yogurt instead of whipped cream, you cut even more fat and cholesterol.

Per Serving:

Calories	213
Total fat	5 g
Saturated fat	1 g
Cholesterol	1 mg
Sodium	61 mg
Carbohydrate	43 g
Fiber	3 g
Protein	3 g

5 cups thinly-sliced peeled apples
1 cup cranberries
2 tablespoons granulated sugar
½ cup quick-cooking rolled oats
⅓ cup packed brown sugar

3 tablespoons all-purpose flour
½ teaspoon ground cinnamon
2 tablespoons margarine
½ cup vanilla or lemon nonfat
   yogurt

In a large mixing bowl combine apples, cranberries, and granulated sugar. Transfer to a 2-quart square baking dish or a 9-inch pie plate.

❧

In a small bowl combine oats, brown sugar, flour, and cinnamon. Cut in margarine till crumbly. Sprinkle oat mixture evenly over apple mixture.

❧

Bake in a 375° oven for 30 to 35 minutes or till apples are tender. Serve warm with a dollop of vanilla or lemon yogurt. Makes 6 servings.

BLUEBERRY COBBLER

By adding orange jucie to the filling, we were able to reduce the sugar content without sacrificing sweetness.

Per Serving:

Calories	174
Total Fat	5 g
Saturated fat	1 g
Cholesterol	<1 mg
Sodium	63 mg
Carbohydrate	32 g
Fiber	2 g
Protein	3 g

⅓ cup sugar
2 tablespoons cornstarch
⅔ cup orange juice
2½ cups fresh or frozen blueberries
½ cup all-purpose flour
½ cup whole wheat flour
1½ teaspoons baking powder
⅓ cup skim milk
3 tablespoons margarine, melted
1 tablespoon sugar
¼ teaspoon ground cinnamon

For filling, in a medium saucepan combine ⅓ cup sugar and cornstarch. Stir in the orange juice. Stir in the blueberries. Cook and stir till thickened and bubbly. Keep filling hot.

For biscuit topping, in a medium mixing bowl combine all-purpose flour, whole wheat flour, and baking powder. Add the milk and margarine; stir just till moistened. On a lightly floured surface pat dough into a 7-inch square; cut into 8 rectangles.

Pour hot filling into a 2-quart square baking dish. Immediately top with biscuit rectangles. Stir together 1 tablespoon sugar and the cinnamon; sprinkle over biscuit rectangles. Bake in a 425° oven for 20 to 25 minutes or till a wooden toothpick inserted into biscuit rectangles comes out clean. Serve warm. Makes 8 servings.

PEACH AND BLUEBERRY CRISP

More fruit and less margarine in the topping make this crisp lighter. Using just a couple tablespoons of toasted pecans gives a pleasant nutty flavor but keeps the fat in check.

25% fewer calories

50% less fat

50% less sodium

2 tablespoons granulated sugar
1 tablespoon all-purpose flour
½ teaspoon ground cinnamon
¼ teaspoon ground nutmeg
4 medium peeled peaches or nectarines, pitted and sliced
1½ cups fresh or frozen blueberries

½ cup quick-cooking or regular rolled oats
⅓ cup packed brown sugar
3 tablespoons all-purpose flour
2 tablespoons margarine
2 tablespoons chopped pecans, toasted
Vanilla ice milk (optional)

Per Serving:

Calories	237
Total fat	6 g
Saturated fat	1 g
Cholesterol	0 mg
Sodium	51 mg
Carbohydrate	46 g
Fiber	4 g
Protein	3 g

For filling, in a small bowl combine granulated sugar, 1 tablespoon flour, cinnamon, and nutmeg. Place the sliced peaches or nectarines and blueberries in a 9-inch pie plate. Sprinkle sugar mixture over fruit. Toss gently to coat fruit with sugar mixture.

For topping, in a small bowl combine oats, brown sugar, and 3 tablespoons flour. Cut in margarine till mixture is crumbly. Stir in toasted pecans. Sprinkle over fruit mixture.

Bake in a 375° oven about 35 minutes or till fruit is tender and center is bubbly. If necessary, cover with foil during last 10 minutes of baking to prevent overbrowning. Serve warm and, if desired, with vanilla ice milk. Makes 6 servings.

Raspberry Kuchen

Nonfat yogurt stands in for cream cheese in the topping of this delicious kuchen.

50% fewer calories

70% less fat

95% less cholesterol

65% less sodium

Nonstick spray coating
1 cup fresh or frozen raspberries
1 cup all-purpose flour
½ cup sugar
1 teaspoon baking powder
¼ cup margarine, melted
¼ cup frozen egg product, thawed
1 teaspoon vanilla

1 8-ounce container plain nonfat yogurt
½ cup sugar
¼ cup frozen egg product, thawed
2 tablespoons all-purpose flour
1½ teaspoons finely shredded lemon peel
1 teaspoon vanilla

Per Serving:

Calories	159
Total fat	4 g
Saturated fat	1 g
Cholesterol	<1 mg
Sodium	73 mg
Carbohydrate	28 g
Fiber	1 g
Protein	3 g

Spray a 9-inch springform pan with nonstick coating; set aside. Thaw frozen raspberries at room temperature for 15 minutes. Drain, if necessary.

In a medium mixing bowl, combine the 1 cup flour, ½ cup sugar, and baking powder. Add margarine, ¼ cup egg product, and 1 teaspoon vanilla. Stir till well mixed. Spread onto bottom of prepared pan; sprinkle with berries.

In a medium mixing bowl combine the yogurt, ½ cup sugar, ¼ cup egg product, 2 tablespoons flour, lemon peel, and 1 teaspoon vanilla. Mix till smooth; pour over berries.

Bake in a 350° oven about 35 minutes or till center appears set when shaken gently. Cool in pan on a wire rack for 15 minutes. Loosen and remove sides of pan. Cool completely. Cover; chill for 2 to 24 hours before serving. Makes 12 servings.

APPLE BREAD PUDDING

Chopped apple, raisins or prunes, and an apple-juice based sauce sweeten this traditional favorite.

Per Serving:

Calories	214
Total fat	5 g
Saturated fat	1 g
Cholesterol	2 mg
Sodium	198 mg
Carbohydrate	37 g
Fiber	1 g
Protein	7 g

3 slices firm-textured whole-grain bread, cut into 1-inch cubes (3½ cups)

1 large apple, peeled, cored, and chopped

2 tablespoons raisins or snipped pitted prunes

1 12-ounce can evaporated skim milk

½ cup frozen egg product, thawed

2 tablespoons sugar

½ teaspoon ground cinnamon

⅛ teaspoon ground nutmeg
    Nutmeg Sauce (see recipe, page 13)

In a 2-quart square baking dish arrange bread cubes, chopped apple, and raisins or prunes.

❧

In a medium mixing bowl combine evaporated skim milk, egg product, sugar, cinnamon, and nutmeg. Beat with an electric mixer on medium speed till well mixed. Pour over bread mixture; let stand for 10 minutes. Cover with foil.

❧

Bake in a 325° oven for 20 minutes. Remove foil; bake for 20 to 25 minutes more or till a knife inserted in center of pudding comes out clean. Cool slightly on wire rack. Serve pudding warm with Nutmeg Sauce. Makes 6 servings.

CHERRY DESSERT DUMPLINGS

Tender and fluffy dumplings steam to perfection in a tart but sweet cherry sauce. Try them warm with a dollop of one of our homemade whipped dessert toppings.

30% fewer calories

30% less sodium

⅔ cup all-purpose flour
2 tablespoons sugar
¾ teaspoon baking powder
⅛ teaspoon ground cinnamon
2 tablespoons margarine
¼ cup frozen egg product, thawed

2 tablespoons skim milk
½ teaspoon vanilla
Tart Cherry Sauce
Whipped Topping or Whipped Milk Topping (see recipes, page 9) (optional)

Per Serving:

Calories	*263*
Total fat	*6 g*
Saturated fat	*1 g*
Cholesterol	*<1 mg*
Sodium	*104 mg*
Carbohydrate	*49 g*
Fiber	*1 g*
Protein	*4 g*

For dumplings, in a medium mixing bowl combine flour, sugar, baking powder, and cinnamon. Cut in margarine till mixture is crumbly. Add egg product, skim milk, and vanilla to flour mixture. Stir just till moistened.

🍃

Heat Tart Cherry Sauce over medium heat to boiling. Drop dumplings into simmering sauce, making 4 dumplings. Reduce heat to medium-low. Cover and cook for 10 to 12 minutes or till a wooden toothpick inserted into dumplings comes out clean. *Do not* remove lid during cooking. Serve warm and, if desired, with a dollop of whipped topping. Makes 4 servings.

TART CHERRY SAUCE: Drain one 16-ounce can *pitted red tart cherries* (water pack), reserving *½ cup* of the liquid. Set aside. In a medium saucepan combine 2 tablespoons *sugar*, 2 tablespoons *cornstarch*, and a dash of *cinnamon*. Stir in reserved ½ cup liquid from cherries, 1 cup *apple juice*, and a few drops *red food coloring*. Cook and stir over medium heat till thickened and bubbly. Stir in cherries.

TORTILLA TORTE

This easy-to-assemble dessert relies on the thick, creamy chocolate sauce and nonfat sour cream for richness and sweetness.

Per Serving:

Calories	149
Total fat	2 g
Saturated fat	1 g
Cholesterol	4 mg
Sodium	140 mg
Carbohydrate	28 g
Fiber	1 g
Protein	4 g

1　8-ounce carton nonfat or light dairy sour cream

1　cup Chocolate Dessert Sauce (see recipe, page 10)

8　8-inch flour tortillas

¼　cup nonfat or light dairy sour cream

1　tablespoon powdered sugar Fresh strawberries, halved (optional)

In a small mixing bowl stir together the 8 ounces of sour cream and the Chocolate Dessert Sauce.

Place 1 tortilla on a serving plate. Spread with *¼ cup* of the chocolate mixture. Top with a second tortilla and more chocolate mixture. Repeat layering with remaining tortillas and chocolate mixture. Cover and chill for 4 to 24 hours.

Before serving, stir together the ¼ cup sour cream and the powdered sugar. Dollop mixture on top of the torte. Serve with fresh strawberries, if desired. Makes 10 servings.

ANY BERRY'S FOOL

This traditional English dessert works with any combination of berries and fruit sauces.
The berries and sauces may be combined for an attractive holiday dessert.

45% fewer calories

65% less fat

95% less cholesterol

1 16-ounce carton vanilla low-fat yogurt
1 8-ounce carton light dairy sour cream
2 teaspoons honey

6 tablespoons Cinnamon Blueberry Sauce or Raspberry Sauce (see recipes, page 12)
¾ cup fresh or frozen blueberries or raspberries

Per Serving:

Calories	*162*
Total Fat	*4 g*
Saturated fat	*2 g*
Cholesterol	*9 mg*
Sodium	*98 mg*
Carbohydrate	*26 g*
Fiber	*1 g*
Protein	*7 g*

Line a strainer with 100% cotton cheesecloth and place over a bowl. Add yogurt. Let drain in refrigerator for 1 to 2 hours or till yogurt measures 1 cup.

In medium bowl combine drained yogurt, sour cream, and honey. Divide yogurt mixture among 6 dessert dishes. Gently fold about *1 tablespoon* of Cinnamon Blueberry Sauce or Raspberry Sauce into each serving of yogurt mixture leaving swirls of fruit and yogurt.

Chill for 2 to 24 hours. Just before serving, top each serving with blueberries or raspberries. Makes 6 servings.

SUMMERTIME BERRY SHORTCAKE

For a summertime dessert, it's hard to beat fresh-picked berries with warm biscuits. Rolled oats add flavor to the reduced-fat biscuits.

⅓ cup rolled oats
1 cup all-purpose flour
1 tablespoon sugar
1 teaspoon baking powder
⅛ teaspoon baking soda
⅓ cup low-fat buttermilk
2 tablespoons cooking oil
  Skim Milk

3 cups blueberries, raspberries, and/or sliced strawberries
2 tablespoons sugar
  Reduced-fat frozen whipped dessert topping, thawed; Whipped Topping (see recipe, page 9); or Whipped Milk Topping (see recipe, page 9)

Per Serving:

Calories	312
Total Fat	9 g
Saturated fat	2 g
Cholesterol	1 mg
Sodium	73 mg
Carbohydrate	54 g
Fiber	4 g
Protein	6 g

In a blender container or food processor bowl, blend or process oats to make oat flour. In a medium mixing bowl stir together oat flour, all-purpose flour, 1 tablespoon sugar, baking powder, and baking soda. Make a well in the center of the dry ingredients. Add buttermilk and oil all at once. Using a fork, stir just till dough clings together.

❧

Turn the dough out onto a lightly floured surface. Quickly knead the dough by gently folding and pressing the dough for 10 to 12 strokes. Pat or lightly roll the dough into a 6-inch square. Cut into four 3-inch squares. Place biscuits on an ungreased baking sheet. Brush lightly with milk.

❧

Bake in a 425° oven about 10 minutes or till golden brown. Remove biscuits from baking sheet and cool on a wire rack for 10 minutes.

❧

Meanwhile, in a medium bowl toss berries with 2 tablespoons sugar. To serve, split warm biscuits in half. Place biscuit bottoms on dessert plates. Top each with some of the berry mixture. Add biscuit tops and remaining berries. Dollop with whipped topping. Serve immediately. Serves 4.

55% fewer calories

85% less fat

no cholesterol

80% less sodium

FRUIT AND BROWNIE PIZZA

This fudgy brownie crust is dense and moist, but low in fat and cholesterol because it's made with chocolate-flavored syrup and frozen egg product.

Per Serving:

Calories	159
Total fat	3 g
Saturated fat	1 g
Cholesterol	0 mg
Sodium	54 g
Carbohydrate	33 g
Fiber	1 g
Protein	2 g

Nonstick spray coating
½ cup sugar
3 tablespoons margarine, softened
¼ cup frozen egg product, thawed
¾ cup chocolate-flavored syrup
⅔ cup all-purpose flour
3 cups sliced, peeled peaches, nectarines, or kiwi fruit; halved strawberries; and/or blueberries
½ cup chocolate-flavored syrup

Spray a 12-inch pizza pan with nonstick coating; set pan aside.

❧

For crust, in a medium mixing bowl combine sugar and margarine. Beat with an electric mixer on medium speed till creamy. Add egg product; beat well. Alternately add the ¾ cup chocolate-flavored syrup and flour, beating after each addition at low speed till combined. Spread mixture in prepared pizza pan.

❧

Bake in a 350° oven for 20 minutes or till top springs back when touched lightly. Cool in pan on a wire rack.

❧

To serve, cut crust into 12 wedges. Top each wedge with some of the fruit. Drizzle each with remaining chocolate-flavored syrup. Makes 12 servings.

APRICOT RICE PUDDING

Made with brown rice and dried fruit, this fiber-rich dessert is a nutritional bargain.

75% less fat

95% less cholesterol

Per Serving:

Calories	*174*
Total Fat	*1 g*
Saturated fat	*< 1 g*
Cholesterol	*3 mg*
Sodium	*111 mg*
Carbohydrate	*34 g*
Fiber	*2 g*
Protein	*7 g*

4   cups skim milk
2   cups cooked quick-cooking
      brown rice
¼   cup sugar
¼   cup snipped dried apricots,
      mixed dried fruit bits, or
      dried cherries
3   inches stick cinnamon
      Dash salt
1   teaspoon vanilla
      Ground nutmeg

In a medium saucepan combine milk; rice; sugar; dried apricots, fruit bits, or cherries; cinnamon; and salt. Bring to boiling. Reduce heat. Cook, uncovered, over low heat for 5 minutes or till mixture thickens slightly, stirring often. Remove from heat. Cool for 10 minutes. Stir in vanilla; remove cinnamon.

Pour into 6 dessert dishes. Sprinkle with nutmeg. Cover and chill in the refrigerator for 2 to 24 hours. Makes 6 servings.

Rosy Rhubarb Parfaits

This bright, flavorful dessert is appealing to the eye, yet low in calories. Chopped peeled peaches, pears, or orange segments could be used instead of strawberries in the gelatin.

35% fewer calories

40% less fat

2 cups diced raw rhubarb
½ cup water
¼ cup sugar
1 4-serving-size package sugar-free strawberry-flavored gelatin
1 teaspoon finely shredded orange peel
½ cup orange juice

½ of an 8-ounce package reduced-fat cream cheese (Neufchâtel), softened
2 tablespoons honey
2 tablespoons skim milk
¼ teaspoon ground nutmeg
1 cup sliced strawberries
  Fresh mint (optional)

Per Serving:

Calories	152
Total fat	5 g
Saturated fat	3 g
Cholesterol	15 mg
Sodium	225 mg
Carbohydrate	21 g
Fiber	2 g
Protein	6 g

In a medium saucepan combine rhubarb, water, and sugar. Heat to boiling. Reduce heat; cover and simmer about 5 minutes or till rhubarb is tender. Remove from heat. Add strawberry gelatin, stirring till gelatin is dissolved. Stir in orange peel and orange juice. Chill till partially set (consistency of unbeaten egg whites).

Meanwhile, in a small bowl combine cream cheese, honey, milk, and nutmeg. Beat till smooth. Cover and chill.

Stir strawberries into thickened gelatin. In 6 parfait glasses alternately layer gelatin mixture and cream cheese mixture. Cover and chill about 4 hours or till set. Garnish with mint, if desired. Makes 6 servings.

CHOCOLATE YOGURT PUDDING

Using low-fat yogurt and unsweetened cocoa powder in this egg-free chocolate pudding reduces the fat and cholesterol to a minimum.

75% less fat

95% less cholesterol

Per Serving:

Calories_____223
Total fat_____2 g
  Saturated fat_____1 g
Cholesterol_____5 mg
Sodium_____83 mg
Carbohydrate_____46 g
Fiber_____<1 g
Protein_____7 g

1 cup sugar
¼ cup unsweetened cocoa
   powder
1 envelope unflavored gelatin
1 12-ounce can evaporated skim
   milk

1 16-ounce carton vanilla low-fat
   yogurt
1 teaspoon vanilla
2 medium bananas, sliced
   Fresh mint (optional)

In a medium saucepan combine sugar, cocoa powder, and gelatin. Gradually stir in evaporated skim milk. Cook and stir over medium heat till mixture comes to a boil and gelatin is dissolved. Cool slightly.

❧

Stir yogurt and vanilla into chocolate mixture. Divide banana slices among 8 dessert dishes. Spoon the chocolate pudding over the banana slices. Cover and chill for 2 to 5 hours or till pudding is set. Garnish with mint, if desired. Makes 8 servings.

BANANA CREAM PARFAITS

These parfaits taste like banana cream pie but by forgoing the pie shell, you save more than 180 calories.

Per Serving:

Calories_____235
Total Fat_____4 g
　Saturated fat_____1 g
Cholesterol_____4 mg
Sodium_____182 mg
Carbohydrate_____43 g
Fiber_____1 g
Protein_____7 g

¼ cup sugar
3 tablespoons all-purpose flour
2¼ cups skim milk
2 teaspoons margarine
1½ teaspoons vanilla
　Few drops yellow food
　　coloring (optional)

2 small bananas
½ cup crushed chocolate wafers
　(about 8 wafers)
2 chocolate wafers (optional)
　Fresh Mint (optional)

For pudding, in a heavy medium saucepan stir together the sugar and flour. Stir in the skim milk all at once. Cook and stir over medium heat till mixture is thickened and bubbly. Cook and stir for 1 minute more. Remove from heat. Stir in margarine, vanilla, and, if desired, food coloring. Spoon pudding into a bowl; cover the surface with plastic wrap. Chill in the refrigerator till serving time.

꙳

To serve, peel and slice bananas; reserve 4 slices for garnish. In 4 parfait glasses, layer *half* of the pudding, the crushed wafers, and the banana slices. Top with remaining pudding. If desired, using a sharp knife, carefully cut the chocolate wafers into quarters. Tuck one piece of chocolate wafer into each serving. Garnish with reserved banana slices. Serve immediately. Makes 4 servings.

CAKES

*It's no surprise that you find lots
of classic angel food cakes here—they've
long been low-calorie favorites that
need little or no modification to fit in a
healthy eating style. But there's more
here…a moist pumpkin gingerbread
served with lemon sauce, squares of glossy
chocolate-glazed chocolate cake,
home-style cakes topped with naturally
sweet plums and peaches, and reduced-egg
sponge cakes. For special occasions,
present the Daffodil Cake, Black Forest
Cake or Meringue-Topped Cake—
all picture-perfect and luscious to eat, too.*

HEAVENLY ANGEL FOOD CAKE

Classic angel food cakes are cholesterol-free and versatile, too. Serve slices plain, with fresh berries, a fresh fruit puree, or in a puddle of chocolate sauce.

1½ cups egg whites
        (10 to 12 large)
1½ cups sifted powdered sugar
1 cup sifted cake flour or sifted
        all-purpose flour

1½ teaspoons cream of tartar
1 teaspoon vanilla
1 cup granulated sugar

Per Serving:

Calories	160
Total fat	<1 g
Saturated fat	<1 g
Cholesterol	0 mg
Sodium	46 mg
Carbohydrate	37 g
Fiber	<1 g
Protein	4 g

Place egg whites in a very large mixing bowl; let stand at room temperature for 30 minutes.

❧

Meanwhile, sift powdered sugar and flour together 3 times. Beat egg whites, cream of tartar, and vanilla with an electric mixer on medium to high speed till soft peaks form (tips curl). Gradually add granulated sugar, about *2 tablespoons* at a time, beating till stiff peaks form (tips stand straight).

❧

Sift about *one-fourth* of the flour mixture over beaten egg whites; fold in gently. Repeat sifting and folding in the remaining flour mixture three more times, using *one-fourth* of the flour mixture each time.

❧

Pour into an *ungreased* 10-inch tube pan. Gently cut through batter with a knife or a narrow metal spatula.

❧

Bake on the lowest rack in a 350° oven for 40 to 45 minutes or till top springs back when lightly touched. (The crust of the cake will be golden and slightly cracked.) Immediately invert the cake in the pan, standing the tube pan on its legs or resting the center tube over a tall-necked bottle. Cool cake thoroughly. Loosen the sides of cake from pan; remove cake from pan. To serve, use a serrated knife to slice the cake into wedges. Makes 12 servings.

PEPPERMINT ANGEL FOOD

This marbled pink angel food cake is also delightful drizzled with chocolate glaze and sprinkled with crushed peppermint candies.

75% less sodium

Per Serving:

Calories	205
Total fat	<1 g
Saturated fat	<1 g
Cholesterol	0 mg
Sodium	67 mg
Carbohydrate	47 g
Fiber	<1 g
Protein	5 g

1⅔ cups egg whites
    (about 12 large)
1 cup sifted powdered sugar
1 cup sifted cake flour or sifted
    all-purpose flour
1½ teaspoons cream of tartar

1 teaspoon vanilla
1 cup granulated sugar
¼ teaspoon peppermint extract
6 drops red food coloring
    Pink Peppermint Frosting

Place egg whites in a very large mixing bowl; let stand at room temperature for 30 minutes.

❧

Sift powdered sugar and flour together 3 times. Beat egg whites, cream of tartar, and vanilla with an electric mixer on medium to high speed till soft peaks form (tips curl). Gradually add granulated sugar, about *2 tablespoons* at a time, beating till stiff peaks form (tips stand straight). Sift about *one-fourth* of the flour mixture over beaten egg whites; fold in gently. Repeat sifting and folding in the remaining flour mixture three more times, using one-fourth of the flour mixture each time.

❧

Divide batter in half. Fold extract and food coloring into one half. Alternately spoon pink and white batters into an *ungreased* 10-inch tube pan. Gently cut through batter with a knife, swirling gently.

❧

Bake on the lowest rack in a 350° oven for 40 to 45 minutes or till top springs back when lightly touched. Immediately invert the cake in the pan, standing the tube pan on its legs or resting the center tube over a tall-necked bottle. Cool thoroughly. Remove cake from pan. Frost with Pink Peppermint Frosting. Store cake leftovers in refrigerator. Makes 12 servings.

PINK PEPPERMINT FROSTING: Place 2 *egg whites* in a bowl. Let stand 30 minutes. In a 2-quart saucepan mix ⅔ cup *sugar*, 2 tablespoons *corn syrup*, and ¼ cup *water*. Cook and stir till mixture comes to a boil. Boil gently, without stirring, for 5 minutes. Beat egg whites using an electric mixer at medium to high speed till soft peaks form (tips curl). Slowly add hot syrup to egg whites, pouring in a steady stream, while beating. Continue beating till stiff glossy peaks form (tips stand straight). Beat in ¼ teaspoon *peppermint extract* and enough *red food coloring* to tint frosting pink.

MOCHA ANGEL LOAF

For chocolate curls, start with a bar of chocolate at room temperature. Carefully pull a vegetable peeler across the chocolate, making thin strips that curl. You can easily pick up the chocolate curls with a toothpick or wooden skewer.

1½ cups egg whites (10 to 12 large)
1½ cups sifted powdered sugar
¾ cup sifted cake flour or sifted all-purpose flour
¼ cup unsweetened cocoa powder
1½ teaspoons cream of tartar
1 cup granulated sugar
1 tablespoon instant coffee granules
⅓ cup cold skim milk
1 1.3-ounce envelope whipped dessert topping mix
½ cup vanilla low-fat yogurt
Chocolate curls or ½ teaspoon unsweetened cocoa powder (optional)

Per Serving:

Calories	211
Total fat	1 g
Saturated fat	<1 g
Cholesterol	1 mg
Sodium	73 mg
Carbohydrate	46 g
Fiber	<1 g
Protein	6 g

Place egg whites in a large mixing bowl; let stand at room temperature for 30 minutes. Line a 15x10x1-inch baking pan with waxed paper; set aside.

❧

Sift powdered sugar, flour, and ¼ cup cocoa powder together 3 times. Beat egg whites and cream of tartar with an electric mixer on medium to high speed till soft peaks form (tips curl). Gradually add granulated sugar, about *2 tablespoons* at a time, beating till stiff peaks form (tips stand straight). Sift about *one-fourth* of the flour mixture over beaten egg whites; fold in gently. Repeat sifting and folding in the remaining flour mixture three more times, using one-fourth of the flour mixture each time. Spread batter in prepared pan.

❧

Bake in a 375° oven for 23 to 25 minutes or till top springs back when lightly touched. Loosen edges. Immediately invert cake onto a large wire rack; remove pan. Carefully peel off waxed paper. Cool thoroughly.

❧

For filling, in bowl dissolve coffee granules in milk; add topping mix. Beat with an electric mixer on low speed till combined. Then beat on high speed till mixture forms stiff peaks (4 to 5 minutes). Fold in yogurt.

❧

To assemble, trim edges from cake. Cut cake crosswise into thirds. Place one cake layer on serving platter; spread with about *one-third* of the filling. Repeat two more times. Cover and refrigerate at least 2 hours or till serving time. Garnish top with chocolate curls or sift cocoa powder over cake, if desired. Makes 10 servings.

CHERRY ALMOND ANGEL FOOD

This light and airy angel cake with bits of bright red cherries and nuts makes any occasion special. Serve plain with a dusting of powdered sugar or a scoop of cherry frozen yogurt.

Per Serving:

Calories	168
Total fat	<1 g
Saturated fat	<1 g
Cholesterol	0 mg
Sodium	56 mg
Carbohydrate	38 g
Fiber	<1 g
Protein	4 g

1⅔ cups egg whites
  (12 large eggs)
1 cup plus 2 tablespoons sifted
  cake flour or sifted all-
  purpose flour
¾ cup sugar

1½ teaspoons cream of tartar
1 teaspoon vanilla
½ teaspoon almond extract
1 cup sugar
10 maraschino cherries, well
  drained and finely chopped

Place egg whites in a very large mixing bowl; let stand at room temperature for 30 minutes.

☙

Sift flour and the ¾ cup sugar together 3 times. Beat egg whites, cream of tartar, vanilla, and almond extract with an electric mixer on medium to high speed till soft peaks form (tips curl). Gradually add the 1 cup sugar, about *2 tablespoons* at a time, beating till soft peaks form (tips stand straight).

☙

Sift about *one-fourth* of the flour mixture over beaten egg whites; fold in gently. Repeat sifting and folding in the remaining flour mixture three more times, using one-fourth of the flour mixture each time. Fold in cherries.

☙

Pour into an *ungreased* 10-inch tube pan. Gently cut through the batter with a knife or narrow metal spatula.

☙

Bake on the lowest rack in a 350° oven for 40 to 45 minutes or till top springs back when lightly touched. (The crust of the cake will be golden and slightly cracked.) Immediately invert the cake in the pan, standing the tube pan on its legs or resting the center tube over a tall-necked bottle. Cool cake thoroughly. Loosen the sides of cake from pan; remove cake from pan. To serve, use a serrated knife to slice the cake into wedges. Makes 12 servings.

DAFFODIL CAKE

40% less fat

40% less cholesterol

50% less sodium

1½ cups egg whites
 (10 to 12 large)
1 cup sifted cake flour or sifted
 all-purpose flour
¾ cup sugar

2 teaspoons vanilla
1½ teaspoons cream of tartar
¾ cup sugar
4 egg yolks
 Lemon Fluff

Per Serving:

Calories	227
Total fat	6 g
Saturated fat	1 g
Cholesterol	71 mg
Sodium	68 mg
Carbohydrate	42 g
Fiber	<1 g
Protein	5 g

Place egg whites in a very large mixing bowl and let stand at room temperature for 30 minutes.

≥•

Sift flour and ¾ cup sugar together 3 times. Beat egg whites, vanilla, and cream of tartar with an electric mixer on medium to high speed till soft peaks form (tips curl). Gradually add ¾ cup sugar, about *2 tablespoons* at a time, beating till stiff peaks form (tips stand straight). Sift about *one-fourth* of the flour mixture over beaten egg whites; fold in gently. Repeat sifting and folding in the remaining flour mixture three more times, using one-fourth of the flour mixture each time. Set egg white mixture aside.

≥•

In a bowl beat egg yolks with an electric mixer on high speed about 5 minutes or till thick and lemon-colored. Divide egg white mixture in half. Fold egg yolk mixture into one portion of the egg white mixture. Alternately spoon yellow and white batters into an *ungreased* 10-inch tube pan. Cut through the batter with a knife or a narrow metal spatula, swirling gently.

≥•

Bake on the lowest rack in a 375° oven for 35 to 40 minutes or till cake springs back when lightly touched near center. Immediately invert the cake in the pan, standing the tube pan on its legs or resting the center tube over a tall-necked bottle. Cool cake thoroughly. Loosen sides of cake from pan; remove cake from pan. Frost with Lemon Fluff. Store cake in refrigerator. Makes 12 servings.

LEMON FLUFF: In a small saucepan combine ¼ cup *sugar* and 1 tablespoon *cornstarch*. Stir in ¾ cup *water*. Cook and stir over medium heat till mixture is thickened and bubbly. Reduce heat. Cook and stir for 2 minutes more. Stir in 1 teaspoon finely shredded *lemon peel*, 1 tablespoon *lemon juice*, and, if desired, 2 to 3 drops *yellow food coloring*. Cover surface with plastic wrap; cool and chill. In a large bowl fold chilled lemon filling into one 8-ounce container reduced-fat frozen *whipped dessert topping*, thawed.

EXTRA-LIGHT CAKE ROLL

Refrigerated reduced-cholesterol whole egg product is a natural alternative for preparing sponge cake roll. If you can't find this product, use whole eggs. Be aware that this cake will not work with a refrigerated egg product made with egg whites.

25% less fat

90% less cholesterol

Per Serving:

Calories	*236*
Total fat	*5 g*
Saturated fat	*3 g*
Cholesterol	*8 mg*
Sodium	*106 mg*
Carbohydrate	*43 g*
Fiber	*<1 g*
Protein	*6 g*

1   cup sifted cake flour or sifted all-purpose flour
1   teaspoon baking powder
¾   cup sugar
½   cup refrigerated reduced-cholesterol whole egg product or 2 eggs
1   teaspoon vanilla
¼   cup water

1   tablespoon sifted powdered sugar
1   quart strawberry frozen yogurt or ice milk, softened
     Sifted powdered sugar (optional)
     Strawberries (optional)
     Orange peel strips (optional)
     Fresh mint (optional)

Line a 15x10x1-inch jelly roll pan with waxed paper; set pan aside.

❧

In a small mixing bowl combine flour and baking powder; set aside.

❧

In a medium mixing bowl beat sugar, whole egg product or eggs, and vanilla with an electric mixer on high speed for 5 minutes or till slightly thick and lemon-colored. Add water and beat on low speed. Sprinkle flour mixture over egg mixture; fold in gently till just combined. Spread batter evenly in prepared jelly-roll pan. Bake in a 375° oven for 12 to 15 minutes or till top is golden and springs back when lightly touched.

❧

Immediately loosen edges of cake from pan and turn cake out onto a towel sprinkled with the 1 tablespoon powdered sugar. Roll up towel and cake, jelly-roll style, starting from one of the cake's short sides. Cool on a wire rack. Unroll cake; remove towel. Spread cake with frozen yogurt or ice milk to within ½ inch of edges. Roll up cake. Wrap and freeze at least 4 hours. Sprinkle with additional powdered sugar before serving, if desired. Garnish with strawberries, orange peel strips, and mint, if desired. Makes 10 servings.

APRICOT-COFFEE SPONGE CAKES

For a potpourri of flavors and color, brush miniature sponge cakes with different flavored preserves, such as pineapple or peach, before arranging on a plate.

Per Cupcake:

Calories	141
Total fat	3 g
Saturated fat	1 g
Cholesterol	36 mg
Sodium	24 mg
Carbohydrate	27 g
Fiber	<1 g
Protein	2 g

Nonstick spray coating
½ cup all-purpose flour
½ teaspoon baking powder
2 eggs
1 teaspoon vanilla
⅔ cup sugar

2 tablespoons water
¼ cup apricot preserves
3 tablespoons finely chopped walnuts, toasted
Coffee Icing

Spray 12 muffin cups with nonstick coating; set aside.

Combine flour and baking powder; set aside. In a large mixing bowl beat eggs and vanilla with an electric mixer on high speed for 4 minutes or till thick. Gradually add sugar, beating at medium speed for 4 to 5 minutes or till light and fluffy. Reduce speed to low; blend in water. Add flour mixture, beating just until combined. Divide batter evenly among prepared muffin cups.

Bake in a 375° oven for 15 minutes or till tops spring back when lightly touched. Remove from pans and cool upside down on wire rack.

In a small saucepan heat apricot preserves till warm. Brush sides of cupcakes with apricot preserves. Place cupcakes upside down on serving plate or wire rack. Prepare Coffee Icing. Pipe or drizzle in a zigzag pattern over cupcakes. Sprinkle with walnuts. Makes 12.

COFFEE ICING: In a small bowl dissolve ½ teaspoon *instant coffee granules* in 1 tablespoon *skim milk*. Add ¾ cup sifted *powdered sugar*, 1 tablespoon softened *margarine*, and ½ teaspoon *vanilla*. Beat with a spoon until smooth. Add additional milk, if necessary to make piping or drizzling consistency.

SIMPLY DELICIOUS CITRUS SPONGE CAKE

A light and refreshing ending to any meal, the springy texture of this sponge cake makes an ideal base for a tangy lemon filling and rainbow topping of fresh fruit.

Per Serving:

Calories	188
Total fat	2 g
Saturated fat	1 g
Cholesterol	80 mg
Sodium	35 mg
Carbohydrate	37 g
Fiber	1 g
Protein	4 g

Nonstick spray coating
3 eggs
⅔ cup sugar
1 teaspoon finely shredded orange peel
1 teaspoon vanilla
⅔ cup sifted cake flour or sifted all-purpose flour
1 cup water
¼ cup sugar
¼ cup refrigerated reduced-cholesterol whole egg product or 1 egg

2 tablespoons cornstarch
1 teaspoon finely shredded lemon peel
2 tablespoons lemon juice
½ teaspoon vanilla
2 tablespoons orange liqueur or orange juice
1½ cups orange sections, blueberries, raspberries, thinly-sliced strawberries, and/or thinly sliced peeled peaches

Spray a 9x1½-inch round baking pan with nonstick coating; set pan aside.

In a medium mixing bowl combine eggs, ⅔ cup sugar, orange peel, and 1 teaspoon vanilla. Beat with an electric mixer on high speed for 5 minutes or till thick and lemon-colored. Fold in flour just till blended. Spread batter in prepared pan.

Bake in a 350° oven for 20 to 25 minutes or till top springs back when touched lightly. Cool in pan on a wire rack for 5 minutes. Carefully remove cake from pan; cool on rack.

For filling, in a small saucepan combine water, ¼ cup sugar, egg product or eggs, and cornstarch. Cook and stir over medium heat till mixture is thickened and bubbly. Cook and stir for 2 minutes more. Remove from heat. Stir in lemon peel, lemon juice, and ½ teaspoon vanilla. Cover surface with plastic wrap. Cool thoroughly.

Carefully cut cake into two horizontal layers. Sprinkle cut surfaces of cake layers with orange liqueur or orange juice. Place *one* layer on serving plate. Spread with *half* of the lemon filling. Place second layer on top and spread with remaining lemon filling. Arrange fruit on top. Cover and chill till serving time. Store any leftover cake in the refrigerator. Makes 8 servings.

SPONGE CAKE

We've reduced the cholesterol and cut the fat of a classic sponge cake by taking out some of the the yolks and adding the egg whites.

3 egg yolks	1½ cups sifted cake flour or
½ cup cold water	1⅓ cups sifted all-purpose
2 teaspoons finely shredded	flour
lemon peel	9 egg whites
1 teaspoon vanilla	¾ teaspoon cream of tartar
¾ cup sugar	¾ cup sugar

Per Serving:

Calories	168
Total fat	1 g
Saturated fat	<1 g
Cholesterol	53 mg
Sodium	44 mg
Carbohydrate	35 g
Fiber	<1 g
Protein	4 g

In a medium mixing bowl beat egg yolks with an electric mixer on high speed about 5 minutes or till thick and lemon-colored. Add water, lemon peel, and vanilla. Beat at low speed till combined. Gradually beat in the ¾ cup sugar. Increase to medium speed; beat till mixture thickens slightly and doubles in volume (about 5 minutes total). Transfer mixture to a very large mixing bowl.

Sprinkle *one-fourth* of the flour over yolk mixture; fold in till combined. Repeat three times with remaining flour, adding one-fourth of the flour at a time. Set aside.

Thoroughly wash beaters. In a large mixing bowl beat egg whites and cream of tartar on medium speed till soft peaks form (tips curl). Gradually add the ¾ cup sugar, beating on high speed till stiff peaks form (tips stand straight).

Fold *1 cup* of the beaten egg white mixture into the yolk mixture; fold yolk mixture into remaining white mixture. Pour into an *ungreased* 10-inch tube pan. Gently cut through the batter with a knife or narrow metal spatula.

Bake in a 325° oven for 55 to 60 minutes or till cake springs back when lightly touched near the center. Immediately invert the cake in the pan, standing the tube pan on its legs or resting the center tube over a tall-necked bottle. Cool cake thoroughly. Loosen sides of cake from pan; remove cake from pan. To serve, use a serrated knife to slice the cake into wedges. Makes 12 servings.

FRUITY CAKE SQUARES

For a change of pace, choose any of the spreadable fruits located with the jellies and preserves in your supermarket. Choose from a wide variety of flavors and colors — apricot, pineapple, strawberry, and raspberry.

60% fewer calories

60% less fat

70% less sodium

Per Serving:

Calories	99
Total fat	2 g
Saturated fat	<1 g
Cholesterol	13 mg
Sodium	25 mg
Carbohydrate	19 g
Fiber	<1 g
Protein	1 g

Nonstick spray coating
1 cup all-purpose flour
1 teaspoon baking powder
1 egg
1 egg white
1 teaspoon finely shredded
   orange peel

1 cup sugar
½ cup skim milk
2 tablespoons margarine
1 9-ounce jar raspberry and
   cranberry spreadable fruit
1 tablespoon powdered sugar

Spray a 9x9x2-inch baking pan with nonstick coating; set pan aside.

Combine flour and baking powder. In a medium mixing bowl beat egg, egg white, and orange peel with an electric mixer on high speed about 4 minutes or till thick. Gradually add sugar, beating at medium speed for 4 to 5 minutes or till light and fluffy. Add flour mixture; beat at low to medium speed just till combined.

In a small saucepan heat and stir milk and margarine till margarine melts. Add milk mixture to batter, beating till combined. Pour into the prepared pan.

Bake in a 350° oven for 20 to 25 minutes or till a wooden toothpick inserted in center comes out clean. Cool cake in pan on wire rack for 10 minutes. Remove cake from pan; cool thoroughly on wire rack.

Carefully cut cake into two horizontal layers. Spread the cut side of one cake layer with spreadable fruit. Place second cake layer on top. Sift powdered sugar over top of cake. Cut into squares. Makes 16 servings.

BOSTON CREAM PIE

This light cake was a favorite in our test kitchens with its creamy filling and shiny chocolate glaze.

Nonstick spray coating
1 cup all-purpose flour
1 teaspoon baking powder
1 egg
1 egg white
1 teaspoon vanilla

1 cup sugar
½ cup skim milk
2 tablespoons margarine
Vanilla Cream Filling
Chocolate Glaze

Per Serving:

Calories	*281*
Total fat	*4 g*
Saturated fat	*1 g*
Cholesterol	*28 mg*
Sodium	*90 mg*
Carbohydrate	*56 g*
Fiber	*<1 g*
Protein	*5 g*

Spray a 9x1½-inch round baking pan with nonstick coating; set pan aside.

❧

Combine flour and baking powder. In a bowl beat egg, egg white, and vanilla with an electric mixer on high speed about 4 minutes or till thick. Gradually add sugar, beating at medium speed 4 to 5 minutes or till light and fluffy. Add flour mixture; beat at low to medium speed just till combined.

❧

In a small saucepan heat and stir milk and margarine till margarine melts. Add milk mixture to batter, beating till combined. Pour into prepared pan.

❧

Bake in a 350° oven for 20 to 25 minutes or till a wooden toothpick inserted near the center comes out clean. Cool cake in pan on wire rack for 10 minutes. Remove cake from pan and cool thoroughly on wire rack. Carefully slice cake into two horizontal layers. Spread chilled Vanilla Cream Filling between the layers. Spread Chocolate Glaze on top. Serves 10.

VANILLA CREAM FILLING: In a heavy medium saucepan combine ⅓ cup *sugar* and 2 tablespoons *cornstarch*. Stir in 1¼ cups *skim milk*. Cook and stir over medium heat till mixture is thickened and bubbly. Cook and stir for 2 minutes more. Remove from heat. Gradually stir about 1 cup of the hot mixture into ¼ cup thawed *frozen egg product*. Return all of the egg mixture to the saucepan. Cook and stir for 2 minutes more. Remove from heat. Stir in 1½ teaspoons *vanilla* and, if desired, 1 to 2 drops *yellow food coloring*. Pour into a bowl. Cover the surface with plastic wrap. Chill

CHOCOLATE GLAZE: In a small mixing bowl stir together ½ cup sifted *powdered sugar*, 1 tablespoon *unsweetened cocoa powder*, 1 tablespoon *skim milk*, and ¼ teaspoon *vanilla* till smooth.

PLUM DELICIOUS CAKE

Not too sweet, this moist cake can also double as a coffee cake—served for breakfast, brunch, or a coffee break.

20% fewer calories

35% less fat

85% less sodium

Nonstick spray coating
1½ cups all-purpose flour
½ cup whole wheat flour
2 teaspoons baking powder
1 teaspoon ground cinnamon
1 cup sugar
⅓ cup cooking oil

1 egg
1 teaspoon vanilla
1 cup skim milk
6 plums, pitted and thinly sliced
1 tablespoon lemon juice
1 tablespoon minced crystallized ginger

Per Serving:

Calories	*172*
Total Fat	*5 g*
Saturated fat	*1 g*
Cholesterol	*14 mg*
Sodium	*15 mg*
Carbohydrate	*29 g*
Fiber	*1 g*
Protein	*3 g*

Spray a 13x9x2-inch baking pan with nonstick coating; set pan aside.

❧

In a medium mixing bowl combine all-purpose flour, whole wheat flour, baking powder, and cinnamon. Set aside. In a large mixing bowl beat sugar and cooking oil with an electric mixer on medium speed till combined. Add the egg and vanilla to sugar mixture; beat on medium speed till creamy, about 1 minute, scraping sides of bowl occasionally. Stir in the milk. With a large spoon, stir dry ingredients into egg mixture. Pour batter into the prepared pan. Arrange plum slices over batter; brush with lemon juice and sprinkle with ginger.

❧

Bake in a 350° oven for 40 to 45 minutes or till a wooden toothpick inserted near the center comes out clean. Cool cake in pan on wire rack. Store leftover cake in the refrigerator. Makes 16 servings.

30% fewer calories

30% less fat

50% less cholesterol

25% less sodium

EASY STRAWBERRY SHORTCAKE

Small amounts of high-fat nuts add lots of flavor to dessert recipes such as this one. For added flavor, we toasted the nuts before mixing into the crumb topping.

Per Serving:

Calories	273
Total fat	13 g
Saturated fat	2 g
Cholesterol	28 mg
Sodium	177 mg
Carbohydrate	39 g
Fiber	1 g
Protein	4 g

Nonstick spray coating
1⅓ cups all-purpose flour
¾ cup packed brown sugar
½ teaspoon baking soda
⅓ cup margarine, softened
1 egg
½ cup low-fat buttermilk

3 tablespoons chopped walnuts, toasted
1 cup reduced-fat frozen whipped dessert topping, thawed
1 pint strawberries, hulled and sliced

Spray a 9-inch round baking pan with nonstick coating; set pan aside.

In a large mixing bowl combine flour, brown sugar, and baking soda. Cut in margarine till crumbly. Remove ½ cup crumb mixture; set aside.

In a small mixing bowl combine egg and buttermilk. Add to crumb mixture, stirring till thoroughly combined. Spread batter into the prepared pan. Sprinkle with reserved crumb mixture and chopped walnuts.

Bake in a 350° oven for 25 to 30 minutes or till a wooden toothpick inserted near the center comes out clean. Cool in pan on a wire rack for 10 minutes. Remove from pan and cool thoroughly on a wire rack. Cut into wedges and serve with a dollop of whipped topping and sliced strawberries. Makes 8 servings.

BLUEBERRY CAKE SQUARES

A great choice for brunch or breakfast because of its moist, tender texture. The toasted wheat germ adds fiber and a nutty flavor.

Per Serving:

Calories	346
Total fat	13 g
Saturated fat	2 g
Cholesterol	24 mg
Sodium	146 mg
Carbohydrate	51 g
Fiber	2 g
Protein	8 g

Nonstick spray coating
2 cups all-purpose flour
½ cup granulated sugar
¼ cup packed brown sugar
¼ cup toasted wheat germ
1¼ teaspoons baking powder
1 teaspoon finely shredded orange peel
½ teaspoon ground cinnamon
¼ teaspoon baking soda
¼ cup skim milk
⅛ teaspoon ground nutmeg

1 egg
2 egg whites
1 8-ounce carton plain nonfat yogurt
⅓ cup cooking oil
1½ cups fresh blueberries or frozen unsweetened blueberries
1 tablespoon all-purpose flour
Crumb Topping
Fresh blueberries (optional)
Fresh mint (optional)

Spray 9x9x2-inch baking pan with nonstick coating; set pan aside.

In a large mixing bowl combine the 2 cups flour, granulated sugar, brown sugar, wheat germ, baking powder, orange peel, cinnamon, baking soda, and nutmeg. In another bowl combine the egg, egg whites, yogurt, and oil. Beat till smooth. Add liquid ingredients to flour mixture, stirring just till combined. Combine 1½ cups blueberries and 1 tablespoon flour; stir into batter. Pour batter into prepared pan. Sprinkle with Crumb Topping.

Bake in a 375° oven for 35 to 40 minutes or till a toothpick inserted near the center comes out clean. Serve warm or cool in pan on a wire rack. Garnish with additional fresh blueberries and mint, if desired. Makes 9 servings.

CRUMB TOPPING: In a small bowl combine ¼ cup chopped *walnuts,* ¼ cup all-purpose *flour,* ¼ cup packed *brown sugar,* and 1 tablespoon melted *margarine.* Mix till crumbly.

PEACHES AND CREAM CAKE

The easiest way to peel peaches is to blanch them in boiling water for about 20 seconds before plunging them into ice water. The peels will slip right off.

Per Serving:

Calories	204
Total Fat	5 g
Saturated fat	1 g
Cholesterol	2 mg
Sodium	76 mg
Carbohydrate	38 g
Fiber	1 g
Protein	4 g

Nonstick spray coating
½ of an 8-ounce container fat-free cream cheese product
1 tablespoon sugar
1 tablespoon orange juice
¾ cup sugar
¼ cup cooking oil
1 egg white
½ teaspoon vanilla

⅓ cup skim milk
1 cup all-purpose flour
1 teaspoon baking powder
2 medium peaches, peeled, pitted, and sliced or 2 cups frozen unsweetened peach slices, thawed
1 tablespoon sugar
¼ teaspoon ground cinnamon

Spray a 10-inch deep-dish pie plate or 10-inch quiche dish with nonstick coating; set aside.

❧

For topping, in a small mixing bowl combine cream cheese product, 1 tablespoon sugar, and orange juice. Beat with an electric mixer on medium speed till smooth; set aside.

❧

In a large mixing bowl combine ¾ cup sugar and oil. Beat with an electric mixer on medium speed till combined. Add egg white and vanilla. Beat till creamy, about 1 minute, scraping sides of bowl occasionally. Stir in milk. Add flour and baking powder. Beat on low speed just till combined, about 1 minute. Pour batter into prepared pie plate. Arrange peach slices over batter. Spoon topping over peaches to within 1 inch of the edge of the pie plate. Combine 1 tablespoon sugar and cinnamon; sprinkle over topping.

❧

Bake in a 350° oven about 40 minutes or till center is set and a wooden toothpick inserted in center of cake comes out clean. (Topping will appear soft.) Cool thoroughly in pie plate on wire rack. Serve at room temperature or cover and chill till serving time. Makes 12 servings.

CORNMEAL PECAN SHORTCAKE

Toasted pecans and lemon peel perk up the flavor of this sweetened shortcake that will bring to mind the flavor of corn muffins.

Nonstick spray coating
1½ cups all-purpose flour
⅓ cup yellow cornmeal
2 teaspoons baking powder
½ teaspoon salt
¾ cup granulated sugar
⅓ cup cooking oil
3 egg whites
1 egg
1 teaspoon vanilla
⅓ cup skim milk
¼ cup finely chopped pecans, toasted
1 teaspoon finely shredded lemon peel
3 cups sliced strawberries
1 tablespoon powdered sugar
1 teaspoon lemon juice
1 8-ounce carton vanilla low-fat yogurt

Per Serving:

Calories	309
Total Fat	12 g
Saturated fat	2 g
Cholesterol	25 mg
Sodium	180 mg
Carbohydrate	45 g
Fiber	2 g
Protein	6 g

Spray a 9x9x2-inch baking pan with nonstick coating; set pan aside.

In a medium bowl combine flour, cornmeal, baking powder, and salt; set aside.

In a large mixing bowl combine granulated sugar and cooking oil. Beat with an electric mixer on medium speed till combined. Add egg whites, egg, and vanilla. Beat till creamy, about 1 minute, scraping sides of bowl occasionally. Stir in milk.

Gradually add flour mixture to egg mixture, stirring till combined. Stir in pecans and lemon peel. Pour batter into prepared pan.

Bake in a 350° oven for 20 to 25 minutes or till a wooden toothpick inserted near the center comes out clean. Cool the cake in the pan on a wire rack for 10 minutes. Remove cake from pan and cool slightly on wire rack.

Meanwhile, in a medium bowl toss together strawberries, powdered sugar, and lemon juice. Cut warm cake into squares. Top with strawberry mixture and vanilla yogurt. Makes 9 servings.

MERINGUE-TOPPED CAKE

We've cut the fat but not the flavor in this version of a classic German cake featuring feather-light yellow cake topped with a soft meringue and filled with a tangy sour cream filling.

	Nonstick spray coating		
1	cup all-purpose flour	⅓	cup skim milk
1½	teaspoons baking powder	3	egg whites
½	cup sugar	⅔	cup sugar
¼	cup margarine, softened	⅓	cup sugar
¼	cup frozen egg product,	1	tablespoon cornstarch
	thawed	1	cup light dairy sour cream
1	teaspoon vanilla	¼	cup frozen egg product,
			thawed

Per Serving:

Calories	260
Total fat	7 g
Saturated fat	2 g
Cholesterol	3 mg
Sodium	122 mg
Carbohydrate	46 g
Fiber	1 g
Protein	5 g

Spray two 8x1½-inch round cake pans with nonstick coating; set pans aside. In a small bowl stir together flour and baking powder; set aside.

In a large mixing bowl combine ½ cup sugar and margarine. Beat with an electric mixer on medium speed till mixture is light and fluffy. Add ¼ cup egg product and vanilla, beating 2 minutes more and scraping bowl often. Add flour mixture alternately with skim milk, beating well on low speed after each addition. Spread batter in prepared pans.

Place egg whites in a medium mixing bowl. Wash beaters thoroughly. Beat egg whites on high speed till frothy. Gradually add ⅔ cup sugar, beating till soft peaks form (tips curl). Carefully spread meringue over batter in both pans.

Bake in a 350° oven for 30 minutes or till meringue is light brown. Cool in pans on wire racks for 10 minutes. Remove from pans. Cool; place layers on racks, meringue side up. Cool completely.

For filling, in medium saucepan combine the ⅓ cup sugar and cornstarch. Stir in sour cream and ¼ cup egg product. Cook and stir over low heat about 5 minutes or till mixture thickens. Cook and stir for 1 minute more. Cool well.

Place one cake layer, meringue side up, on a serving plate. Spread with filling. Top with the other cake layer, meringue side up. Cover cake and chill till serving time. Makes 10 servings.

MARBLE CAKE

For this makeover of marble pound cake, we substituted egg product and egg whites for whole eggs, cocoa for chocolate, and halved the margarine.

Nonstick spray coating
2 cups all-purpose flour
2 teaspoons baking powder
⅛ teaspoon salt
2 cups sugar
½ cup margarine, softened
¼ cup frozen egg product, thawed
¾ cup skim milk
1 teaspoon almond extract
4 egg whites
1 tablespoon skim milk
⅓ cup unsweetened cocoa powder, sifted
1 tablespoon powdered sugar

Spray a 10-inch fluted tube pan with nonstick coating; set pan aside. In a small mixing bowl stir together flour, baking powder, and salt; set aside.

In a large mixing bowl combine sugar and margarine. Beat with an electric mixer on high speed till combined. Add egg product and beat on medium speed till smooth.

Gradually add flour mixture alternately with the ¾ cup skim milk to sugar mixture, beating well after each addition. Add almond extract.

Wash and dry the beaters. In a medium mixing bowl beat the egg whites on high speed till stiff peaks form (tips stand straight). Fold into batter. Pour *half* of the batter into prepared pan. Stir 1 tablespoon milk into remaining batter; add cocoa powder, stirring till smooth. Pour chocolate batter over batter in pan. Gently cut through the batter with a knife or narrow metal spatula, swirling gently to marble.

Bake in a 350° oven for 40 to 45 minutes or till a wooden toothpick inserted near the center comes out clean. Cool cake in pan on a wire rack for 10 minutes. Remove cake from pan and cool thoroughly on a wire rack. Sift powdered sugar over cake before serving. Makes 16 servings.

BLACK FOREST CAKE

Attractive and full of flavor, too, this chocolate cake is a crowd-pleaser with only one gram of saturated fat and less than one milligram of cholesterol per serving.

Per Serving:

Calories	222
Total Fat	12 g
Saturated fat	1 g
Cholesterol	<1 mg
Sodium	75 mg
Carbohydrate	28 g
Fiber	<1 g
Protein	3 g

Nonstick spray coating
1¼ cups all-purpose flour
⅔ cup sugar
¼ cup unsweetened cocoa powder
½ teaspoon baking soda
1 cup water
⅓ cup cooking oil

1 tablespoon white vinegar
1 teaspoon vanilla
2 egg whites
1½ cups reduced-fat frozen whipped dessert topping, thawed
1 cup reduced-calorie cherry pie filling

Spray a 9x1½-inch round baking pan with nonstick coating; set pan aside.

❧

In a medium mixing bowl combine flour, sugar, cocoa powder, and baking soda. Add water, cooking oil, vinegar, and vanilla. Stir till thoroughly combined.

❧

In a medium mixing bowl beat the egg whites with an electric mixer on high speed till stiff peaks form (tips stand straight). Fold into batter Pour batter into the prepared baking pan.

❧

Bake in a 350° oven about 25 minutes or till wooden toothpick inserted near the center comes out clean. Cool cake in pan on wire rack for 10 minutes. Remove cake from pan and cool thoroughly on wire rack. Spread whipped dessert topping over top and sides of cooled cake. Top with pie filling. Makes 8 servings.

CHOCOLATE COCONUT CAKE

If you're not a coffee drinker, substitute 1 teaspoon instant coffee granules and ½ cup water for the brewed coffee.

Per Serving:

Calories	205
Total fat	9 g
Saturated fat	2 g
Cholesterol	18 mg
Sodium	92 mg
Carbohydrate	30 g
Fiber	1 g
Protein	3 g

Nonstick spray coating
1 cup all-purpose flour
1 cup sugar
⅓ cup unsweetened cocoa powder
1 teaspoon baking powder
½ teaspoon baking soda
1 egg
½ cup low-fat buttermilk
½ cup strong coffee
¼ cup cooking oil
1 teaspoon vanilla
Coconut Topping

Spray a 9x9x2-inch baking pan with nonstick coating; set pan aside. In a medium mixing bowl combine flour, sugar, cocoa powder, baking powder, and baking soda. Add egg, buttermilk, coffee, oil, and vanilla. Beat with an electric mixer on medium speed till thoroughly combined. Pour batter into the prepared pan.

❧

Bake in a 350° oven about 30 minutes or till a wooden toothpick inserted near the center comes out clean. Meanwhile, prepare Coconut Topping. Carefully spread Coconut Topping on hot cake. Broil about 5 inches from the heat for 1 to 2 minutes or until coconut is lightly browned. Cool in pan on a wire rack. Cut cake into squares with a wet knife. Makes 12 servings.

COCONUT TOPPING: In a small mixing bowl combine ½ cup *coconut*, ¼ cup packed *brown sugar*, 2 tablespoons melted *margarine*, and 2 tablespoons *skim milk*. Stir to mix well.

SPICY COFFEE SQUARES

If you don't have any apple pie spice, make your own with 1 teaspoon ground cinnamon and ¼ teaspoon each ground ginger and ground nutmeg.

Nonstick spray coating
1½ cups sifted cake flour or 1⅓ cups all-purpose flour
1½ teaspoons apple pie spice
1 teaspoon baking powder
¼ teaspoon baking soda
¾ cup packed brown sugar
⅓ cup margarine, softened
1 egg white or 2 tablespoons frozen egg product, thawed
½ cup hot brewed coffee
1 tablespoon powdered sugar

Per Serving:

Calories	*202*
Total fat	*7 g*
Saturated fat	*1 g*
Cholesterol	*0 mg*
Sodium	*116 mg*
Carbohydrate	*33 g*
Fiber	*1 g*
Protein	*2 g*

Spray a 9x9x2-inch baking pan with nonstick coating; set pan aside. In a small mixing bowl stir together flour, apple pie spice, baking powder, and baking soda; set aside.

In a medium mixing bowl combine brown sugar and margarine. Beat with an electric mixer on medium to high speed till smooth. Add egg white or egg product and beat till smooth.

Add flour mixture alternately with hot coffee to sugar mixture, beating on low speed after each addition. Pour batter into prepared pan.

Bake in a 350° oven about 25 minutes or till cake pulls slightly away from sides of pan and a wooden toothpick inserted in center comes out clean. *Do not* overbake. Cool in pan on a wire rack for 15 to 20 minutes or till warm. Sift powdered sugar over warm cake. Serve warm or cool. Makes 9 servings.

OLD-FASHIONED PUMPKIN GINGERBREAD

To decorate this cake without adding many calories, secure a paper doily on top of the cake with toothpicks. Sift powdered sugar over the surface and then carefully remove the doily and the toothpicks.

50% less fat

no cholesterol

Per Serving:

Calories	*251*
Total fat	*6 g*
Saturated fat	*1 g*
Cholesterol	*0 mg*
Sodium	*242 mg*
Carbohydrate	*49 g*
Fiber	*1 g*
Protein	*3 g*

Nonstick spray coating
1¼ cups sifted cake flour or sifted all-purpose flour
1 teaspoon baking soda
½ teaspoon baking powder
½ teaspoon ground cinnamon
½ teaspoon ground ginger
¼ teaspoon salt
½ cup packed brown sugar
¼ cup margarine, softened
2 tablespoons granulated sugar
1½ teaspoons finely shredded orange peel
3 egg whites
1 cup canned pumpkin
¼ cup light corn syrup
2 tablespoons molasses
1 tablespoon powdered sugar
Orange Sauce (see recipe, page 10)

Spray an 8x8x2-inch baking pan with nonstick coating; set pan aside. In a small mixing bowl stir together flour, baking soda, baking powder, cinnamon, ginger, and salt; set aside.

❧

In a large mixing bowl combine brown sugar, margarine, granulated sugar, and orange peel. Beat with an electric mixer on medium to high speed till smooth. Add egg whites, one at a time, beating about 1 minute after each addition. Add pumpkin, corn syrup, and molasses, beating on low speed till smooth.

❧

Gradually add flour mixture to sugar mixture, beating at low speed just till combined. Pour batter into prepared pan.

❧

Bake in a 350° oven about 30 minutes or till a wooden toothpick inserted in center comes out clean. Do not overbake. Cool cake in pan on a wire rack about 15 minutes. Sprinkle with powdered sugar. Serve warm or cool with Orange Sauce. Makes 9 servings.

APPLE BUTTER CAKE

Apple butter adds moistness to this easy-to-make spice cake. The thin lemon glaze adds a delightful flavor perfect for a mid-morning coffee break.

Per Serving:

Calories	*171*
Total fat	*4 g*
Saturated fat	*1 g*
Cholesterol	*13 mg*
Sodium	*96 mg*
Carbohydrate	*34 g*
Fiber	*1 g*
Protein	*2 g*

Nonstick spray coating
1½ cups all-purpose flour
½ teaspoon baking soda
½ teaspoon baking powder
½ teaspoon ground cinnamon
¼ teaspoon ground nutmeg
⅛ teaspoon ground cloves

¾ cup sugar
¼ cup margarine, softened
1 egg
2 egg whites
2 teaspoons finely shredded lemon peel
1 cup apple butter
Lemon Icing

Spray a 13x9x2-inch baking pan with nonstick coating; set pan aside. In a medium bowl combine flour, baking soda, baking powder, cinnamon, nutmeg, and cloves; set aside.

❧

In a large mixing bowl combine sugar and margarine. Beat with an electric mixer on medium speed till combined. Add egg, egg whites, and lemon peel; beat till smooth. Add apple butter alternately with dry ingredients, beating on low speed after each addition just till mixed. Spread batter in prepared pan.

❧

Bake in a 350° oven for 25 to 30 minutes or till a wooden toothpick inserted near the center comes out clean. Cool in pan on a rack.Drizzle Lemon Icing over cooled cake. To serve, cut into squares. Makes 16 servings.

LEMON ICING: In a small mixing bowl combine 1 cup sifted *powdered sugar*, 1 teaspoon finely shredded *lemon peel*, and 4 teaspoons *milk*. Stir till smooth, adding additional milk if necessary to make icing into drizzling consistency.

HONEY-GLAZED YOGURT CAKE

Pipe thawed frozen whipped topping around edge of the glazed cake with a large star tip.
Then decorate with bits of apricots and prunes, and some fine orange peel strips.

45% less fat

25% less sodium

Per Serving:

Calories	*305*
Total fat	*7 g*
Saturated fat	*1 g*
Cholesterol	*22 mg*
Sodium	*150 mg*
Carbohydrate	*56 g*
Fiber	*1 g*
Protein	*6 g*

Nonstick spray coating
2 cups all-purpose flour
1½ teaspoons baking powder
½ teaspoon baking soda
¾ cup sugar
¼ cup margarine, softened
1 teaspoon vanilla
1 egg
1 egg white
1 8-ounce carton plain nonfat yogurt

¼ cup skim milk
¼ cup snipped dried apricots
¼ cup snipped prunes
¼ cup finely chopped walnuts or pecans
Orange-Honey Glaze
Reduced-fat frozen whipped dessert topping, thawed, or Whipped Topping or Whipped Milk Topping (see recipes, page 9) (optional)

Spray a 9-inch springform pan with nonstick coating; set pan aside. In a medium bowl combine flour, baking powder, and baking soda; set aside.

In a large mixing bowl combine sugar, margarine, and vanilla. Beat with an electric mixer on medium speed till well combined. Add egg and egg white; beat 2 minutes at medium speed. Combine yogurt and milk. Add flour mixture alternately with yogurt mixture, beating at low speed just till mixed after each addition. Stir in apricots, prunes, and nuts. Spread batter in prepared pan. Place pan on baking sheet.

Bake in a 350° oven for 40 to 45 minutes or till a wooden toothpick inserted near the center comes out clean. Cool cake in pan on a wire rack.

Meanwhile, prepare Orange Honey Glaze. Pierce entire top surface of cake with a fork. Spoon warm Orange Honey Glaze over cake. Cool for 30 minutes more. Remove sides of pan. Cool completely.

To serve, cut into wedges. Top each wedge with whipped topping additional apricots and prunes, and orange peel, if desired. Makes 10 servings.

ORANGE-HONEY GLAZE: In a small saucepan combine ½ cup *honey*, 1 teaspoon finely shredded *orange peel*, and ½ cup *orange juice*. Heat just to boiling, stirring occasionally. Remove from heat.

HONEY-GLAZED ALMOND CAKE

Finely ground almonds and wheat germ add rich flavor to this dense cake. Brushing the cake with honey keeps it moist.

Nonstick spray coating
⅔ cup sugar
½ cup all-purpose flour
½ cup sliced almonds
3 tablespoons wheat germ
4 egg whites

1 teaspoon vanilla
¼ teaspoon almond extract
¼ cup margarine, melted
1 tablespoon honey
  Whipped Topping or Whipped Milk Topping (see recipes, page 9)

Spray an 8x1½-inch round cake pan with nonstick coating; set pan aside. In a food processor bowl container combine sugar, flour, almonds, and wheat germ. Cover and process till almonds are finely ground. (For a blender, in a bowl combine almonds, sugar, flour, and wheat germ. Add mixture to blender container *one-third* at a time and blend till almonds are finely ground.)

❧

In a large mixing bowl beat egg whites, vanilla, and almond extract with an electric mixer on high speed till stiff peaks form (tips stand straight). (*Do not* overbeat.) By hand gently fold in the almond mixture. Then fold in melted margarine. Spread the batter in the prepared cake pan.

❧

Bake in a 375° oven for 25 to 30 minutes or till a wooden toothpick inserted near the center comes out clean. Cool in pan on a wire rack for 10 minutes; remove from pan. Drizzle hot cake with honey.

❧

Serve warm or cool with whipped topping, if desired. Makes 8 servings.

BANANA CRUMB CAKE

If you'd like to transform this moist snack cake into cupcakes, spoon the batter into 15 muffin cups lined with paper baking cups. Sprinkle with the Crumb Topping and bake for 20 to 25 minutes.

	Nonstick spray coating
1	teaspoon all-purpose flour
2	cups all-purpose flour
½	teaspoon baking powder
½	teaspoon baking soda
1	cup sugar
⅓	cup margarine, softened
1	egg

2	egg whites
¼	cup low-fat buttermilk
1	teaspoon vanilla
1	cup mashed ripe banana
	Crumb Topping
⅓	cup sifted powdered sugar
1	teaspoon skim milk

Per Serving:

Calories	258
Total fat	7 g
Saturated fat	1 g
Cholesterol	18 mg
Sodium	132 mg
Carbohydrate	46 g
Fiber	1 g
Protein	4 g

Spray a 9x9x2-inch baking pan with nonstick coating. Dust lightly with the 1 teaspoon flour. Set pan aside. In a small bowl stir together flour, baking powder, and baking soda; set aside.

In a large mixing bowl combine sugar and margarine. Beat with an electric mixer at medium speed till light and fluffy. Add egg, egg whites, buttermilk, and vanilla. Beat till well mixed. Add flour mixture, beating till thoroughly combined. Stir in mashed banana. Pour batter into prepared pan. Sprinkle with Crumb Topping.

Bake in a 350° oven for 30 to 35 minutes or till a wooden toothpick inserted in the center comes out clean. Cool in pan on a wire rack.

For icing, stir together powdered sugar and skim milk. Drizzle over cake. Makes 12 servings.

CRUMB TOPPING: In a small bowl combine ¼ cup *all-purpose flour*, ¼ cup packed *brown sugar*, and ⅛ teaspoon ground *cinnamon*. Add 1 tablespoon *cooking oil*, stirring with a fork till mixture is crumbly.

CHOCOLATE SHEET CAKE

This glazed moist cake will appeal to any chocolate lover. It's simply delicious and easy to make with a handy one-bowl method.

Per Serving:

Calories:	*248*
Total Fat:	*7 g*
Saturated fat:	*1 g*
Cholesterol:	*14 mg*
Sodium:	*139 mg*
Carbohydrate:	*44 g*
Fiber:	*<1 g*
Protein:	*3 g*

Nonstick spray coating
1 teaspoon all-purpose flour
2 cups all-purpose flour
2 cups sugar
1 teaspoon baking soda
1⅓ cups water
½ cup margarine
⅓ cup unsweetened cocoa powder
½ cup low-fat buttermilk
2 egg whites
1 egg
1½ teaspoons vanilla
Chocolate Glaze

Spray a 13x9x2-inch baking pan with nonstick coating and dust lightly with flour; set pan aside.

In a large mixing bowl combine 2 cups flour, sugar, and baking soda. In a medium saucepan combine water, margarine, and cocoa powder. Bring just to boiling, stirring constantly. Remove from heat. Add to dry ingredients. Beating with an electric mixer on low speed just till combined. Add buttermilk, egg whites, egg, and vanilla. Beat for 1 minute. (Batter will be thin). Pour into prepared pan.

Bake in a 350° oven for 25 to 30 minutes or till a wooden toothpick inserted in the center comes out clean. Cool cake in pan on wire rack. Spread Chocolate Glaze over cake. Let stand till set. Makes 16 servings.

CHOCOLATE GLAZE: In a small mixing bowl stir together 1 cup sifted *powdered sugar*, 2 tablespoons *unsweetened cocoa powder*, 2 tablespoons *skim milk*, and ½ teaspoon *vanilla* till smooth.

Chocolate Cream Cheese Cupcakes

These "surprise" cupcakes are lighter than fudge cake spread with cream cheese frosting. Instead, the cupcakes are filled with a fat-free cream cheese and frozen egg product mixture.

40% fewer calories

45% less fat

45% less sodium

½ cup fat-free cream cheese product

¼ cup frozen egg product, thawed

⅓ cup sugar

⅓ cup miniature semisweet chocolate pieces

1½ cups all-purpose flour

1 cup sugar

¼ cup unsweetened cocoa powder

1 teaspoon baking powder

¼ teaspoon baking soda

⅛ teaspoon salt

1 cup water

⅓ cup cooking oil

1 tablespoon vinegar

1 teaspoon vanilla

¼ cup chopped walnuts

Per Cupcake:

Calories	*159*
Total Fat	*7 g*
Saturated fat	*1 g*
Cholesterol	*1 mg*
Sodium	*80 mg*
Carbohydrate	*22 g*
Fiber	*1 g*
Protein	*3 g*

Line 18 muffin cups with paper bake cups.

In a small mixing bowl beat cream cheese product with an electric mixer on medium speed till smooth. Add egg product and ⅓ cup sugar. Beat on medium speed for 1 minute or till smooth. Stir in semisweet chocolate pieces; set aside.

In a large mixing bowl combine flour, 1 cup sugar, cocoa powder, baking powder, baking soda, and salt. Add water, oil, vinegar, and vanilla. Beat with an electric mixer on medium speed for 2 minutes, scraping sides of the bowl occasionally. Spoon the batter into prepared muffin cups, filling *half* full. Spoon about *1 tablespoon* of cream cheese mixture over each. Sprinkle with walnuts.

Bake in a 350° oven for 25 to 30 minutes or till a wooden toothpick inserted near the center of a cupcake comes out clean. Cool cupcakes in pan on wire rack for 10 minutes. Remove cupcakes from pan; cool thoroughly on a wire rack. Makes 18 cupcakes.

DOUBLE LEMON CUPCAKES

Light, lemony, and bursting with flavor, a little yellow food coloring gives these cupcakes a brighter color.

Per Cupcake:

Calories	188
Total fat	4 g
Saturated fat	1 g
Cholesterol	<1 mg
Sodium	64 mg
Carbohydrate	36 g
Fiber	<1 g
Protein	2 g

Nonstick spray coating
1⅓ cups all-purpose flour
2 teaspoons baking powder
2 teaspoons finely shredded lemon peel
⅛ teaspoon ground nutmeg
½ cup sugar
¼ cup margarine, softened
⅔ cup skim milk
2 to 3 drops yellow food coloring (optional)
2 egg whites
¼ cup sugar
Lemon Icing

Spray 12 muffin cups with nonstick coating or line with paper bake cups. Set pan aside. In a small bowl combine flour, baking powder, lemon peel, and nutmeg; set aside.

In a large mixing bowl combine ½ cup sugar and margarine. Beat with an electric mixer on medium speed till light and fluffy. Add flour mixture alternately with skim milk, beating on low speed after each addition. If desired, beat in food coloring.

Wash and dry beaters. In a small mixing bowl beat egg whites on medium speed till soft peaks form (tips curl). Gradually add the ¼ cup sugar, beating on high speed till stiff peaks form (tips stand straight). Stir some of the beaten egg whites into batter to lighten. Gently fold remaining beaten egg whites into batter. Spoon batter into prepared muffin cups, filling *three-fourths* full.

Bake in a 350° oven for 15 to 18 minutes or till a wooden toothpick inserted in the centers comes out clean. Cool in pans on wire rack for 10 minutes. Remove from pan; cool completely on wire racks. Frost with Lemon Icing. Makes 12.

LEMON ICING: In a small bowl combine 1½ cups sifted *powdered sugar*, ½ teaspoon finely shredded *lemon peel*, and enough *lemon juice* to make icing of spreading consistency (1 to 2 tablespoons).

CRANBERRY-ORANGE CAKE

This moist, fruited cake combines ruby-red, tangy cranberries with the sweetness of oranges.
Great for packing in lunch boxes or taking on a picnic.

Nonstick spray coating
1 teaspoon all-purpose flour
2 cups all-purpose flour
1 cup sugar
1½ teaspoons baking powder
½ teaspoon baking soda
1 egg
¼ cup cooking oil

1 tablespoon finely shredded orange peel
¾ cup orange juice
1 cup coarsely chopped cranberries
¼ cup finely chopped almonds, toasted
1 tablespoon all-purpose flour
1 tablespoon powdered sugar

Per Serving:

Calories	215
Total fat	7 g
Saturated fat	1 g
Cholesterol	18 mg
Sodium	42 mg
Carbohydrate	36 g
Fiber	1 g
Protein	3 g

Spray an 8x8x2-inch baking pan with nonstick coating. Dust with 1 teaspoon flour; set pan aside.

In a large mixing bowl combine 2 cups flour, sugar, baking powder, and baking soda. In another bowl combine egg, oil, orange peel, and orange juice; mix well. Add egg mixture to flour mixture, stirring just till combined. Toss together cranberries, almonds, and 1 tablespoon flour. Stir into batter. Pour batter into prepared baking pan.

Bake in a 350° oven about 40 minutes or till a wooden toothpick inserted in the center comes out clean. Cool in pan on a wire rack for 10 minutes. Remove from pan; cool completely on rack. Sift powdered sugar over cooled cake. Makes 12 servings.

COOKIES

*W*hether you choose tasty old-fashioned
cookies such as Chewy Molasses Ginger
Cookies or melt-in-your-mouth meringues
such as Peppermint Stars, you'll find all
these recipes easy to prepare and fun to
eat. Our Blondie Bars are a fine substitute
for high-calorie chocolate chip cookies and
are one of many bar cookies from which
to choose. Chocolate lovers won't be able
to resist the cake-like Raspberry Brownies
sprinkled with powdered sugar and
drizzled with chocolate icing.

BLONDIE BARS

Reducing the fat in an American classic like chocolate chip cookies wasn't easy. We've added some applesauce for moisture and baked them in bars instead of drop cookies.

20% less fat

Nonstick spray coating
½ cup margarine, softened
½ cup granulated sugar
½ cup packed brown sugar
1 teaspoon baking soda
½ cup unsweetened applesauce

1 egg
1 teaspoon vanilla
2¼ cups all-purpose flour
¾ cup miniature semisweet chocolate pieces

Per Cookie:

Calories	91
Total Fat	4 g
Saturated fat	1 g
Cholesterol	6 mg
Sodium	55 mg
Carbohydrate	14 g
Fiber	< 1 g
Protein	1 g

Spray a 13x9x2-inch baking pan with nonstick coating; set pan aside.

In a large mixing bowl beat the margarine with an electric mixer on medium to high speed for 30 seconds. Add the granulated sugar, brown sugar, and baking soda. Beat mixture till thoroughly combined, scraping the sides of the bowl occasionally. Beat in the applesauce, egg, and vanilla. Beat in as much of the flour as you can with the mixer. Stir in any remaining flour with a wooden spoon. Stir in the chocolate pieces. Spread dough into the prepared baking pan.

Bake in a 350° oven for 20 to 25 minutes or till light brown and a wooden toothpick inserted in center comes out clean. Cool thoroughly in pan on wire rack. Cut into bars. Makes 36.

RASPBERRY BROWNIES

These classic brownies have been made healthier by eliminating egg yolk, reducing the margarine, and adding evaporated skim milk. Fresh raspberries add a delicious twist.

Per Cookie:

Calories	195
Total fat	5 g
Saturated fat	1 g
Cholesterol	14 mg
Sodium	65 mg
Carbohydrate	35 g
Fiber	1 g
Protein	3 g

Nonstick spray coating
1¼ cups all-purpose flour
1 cup granulated sugar
½ cup packed brown sugar
½ cup unsweetened cocoa
    powder
⅓ cup margarine, melted
⅓ cup evaporated skim milk
2 egg whites
1 egg
2 tablespoons light corn syrup
1 tablespoon raspberry liqueur
    or orange juice
1 teaspoon vanilla
¾ cup fresh raspberries
1 tablespoon powdered sugar
    Chocolate-Raspberry Glaze

Spray a 9x9x2-inch baking pan with nonstick coating; set pan aside.

In a large bowl combine the flour, granulated sugar, brown sugar, and cocoa powder. Make a well in the center. Add the melted margarine, evaporated skim milk, egg whites, egg, corn syrup, raspberry liqueur or orange juice, and vanilla. Beat with a spoon till well mixed. Spread the batter into the prepared baking pan. Sprinkle raspberries on top.

Bake in a 350° oven for 40 minutes. Cool in pan on a wire rack. Sift powdered sugar over top. Drizzle with Chocolate-Raspberry Glaze. Let stand about 30 minutes or till glaze is set. Cut into bars. Makes 16.

CHOCOLATE-RASPBERRY GLAZE: In small bowl stir together ½ cup *powdered sugar*, 1 tablespoon *unsweetened cocoa powder*, 1 tablespoon *raspberry liqueur or orange juice*, and ¼ teaspoon *vanilla* to make a glaze of drizzling consistency. If necessary, add 1 to 2 teaspoons *water*.

APPLESAUCE SPICE BARS

When you taste these bars you won't miss the fat because the molasses and applesauce keep them moist, the spice blend is just right, and the lemon glaze adds sweetness.

25% fewer calories

75% less fat

Per Cookie:

Calories	67
Total fat	1 g
Saturated fat	<1 g
Cholesterol	<1 mg
Sodium	27 mg
Carbohydrate	13 g
Fiber	<1 g
Protein	1 g

Nonstick spray coating
2   cups all-purpose flour
2   teaspoons baking powder
1   teaspoon baking soda
½   teaspoon ground cinnamon
½   teaspoon ground nutmeg
¼   teaspoon ground cloves
¼   cup margarine, softened
½   cup sugar
1   cup unsweetened applesauce
½   cup frozen egg product, thawed
½   cup molasses
½   cup raisins
    Lemon Glaze

Spray a 15x10x1-inch baking pan with nonstick coating; set pan aside. In a bowl stir together flour, baking powder, baking soda, cinnamon, nutmeg, and cloves; set aside.

🍂

In a large mixing bowl beat margarine with an electric mixer on medium to high speed for 30 seconds. Add sugar and beat till thoroughly combined. Beat in applesauce, egg product, and molasses till combined.

🍂

Add flour mixture to molasses mixture and beat at low speed till combined. (Mixture may appear lumpy.) Stir in raisins. Spread batter in prepared pan.

🍂

Bake in a 350° oven about 20 minutes or till a wooden toothpick inserted near the center comes out clean. Cool in pan on a wire rack. Drizzle with Lemon Glaze. Cut into bars. Makes 48.

LEMON GLAZE: In a small bowl stir together 1½ cups sifted *powdered sugar*, 2 tablespoons *skim milk*, 1 teaspoon finely shredded *lemon peel*, and 2 teaspoons *lemon juice* till smooth and of drizzling consistency.

FRUITY APRICOT-GINGER BARS

This old-fashioned bar cookie is always a favorite. We cut the fat and the sugar so there's no reason to hide them from the children or yourself.

45% fewer calories

30% less fat

45% less sodium

Nonstick spray coating
⅔ cup all-purpose flour
⅔ cup regular or quick-cooking rolled oats
⅓ cup packed brown sugar
½ teaspoon ground cinnamon
¼ teaspoon baking soda

¼ cup margarine
¾ cup low-sugar apricot spread
1½ teaspoons grated gingerroot or ¼ teaspoon ground ginger
2 tablespoons finely chopped walnuts or pecans

Per Cookie:

Calories	98
Total Fat	4 g
Saturated fat	1 g
Cholesterol	0 mg
Sodium	54 mg
Carbohydrate	15 g
Fiber	< 1 g
Protein	1 g

Spray an 8x8x2-inch baking pan with nonstick coating; set pan aside.

❧

In a mixing bowl combine flour, oats, brown sugar, cinnamon, and baking soda. Cut in margarine till mixture resembles coarse crumbs. Reserve ⅓ *cup* of the crumb mixture. Press remaining crumb mixture into bottom of prepared baking pan. Combine apricot spread and ginger. Carefully spread apricot mixture over flour mixture in pan. Combine nuts with reserved crumb mixture. Sprinkle over apricot mixture.

❧

Bake in a 350° oven for 25 to 30 minutes or till top is golden. Cool in the pan on a wire rack. Cut into bars. Makes 16.

DATE BARS WITH ORANGE ICING

There's almost no fat in these bar cookies which rely on dates for moistness. The orange icing adds a sweet note that balances all the flavors.

25% fewer calories

75% less fat

Nonstick spray coating
1 cup all-purpose flour
1 teaspoon baking powder
½ teaspoon ground cinnamon
¼ teaspoon baking soda
½ cup snipped dates
2 eggs

1 cup packed brown sugar
¾ cup evaporated skim milk
¼ cup finely chopped walnuts, toasted
Orange Icing
Thin strips of orange peel (optional)

Per Cookie:

Calories	*61*
Total fat	*1 g*
Saturated fat:	*<1 g*
Cholesterol:	*9 mg*
Sodium:	*20 mg*
Carbohydrate:	*12 g*
Fiber:	*<1 g*
Protein:	*<1 g*

Spray a 15x10x1-inch baking pan with nonstick coating; set pan aside. In a small bowl combine flour, baking powder, cinnamon, and baking soda.

Place dates in a small bowl and pour 1 cup *boiling water* over them. Let stand for 10 minutes. Drain well.

In a small mixing bowl beat eggs with an electric mixer on high speed till frothy. Add brown sugar and dates, beating till mixture is well combined. Stir in evaporated skim milk.

Add flour mixture to egg mixture, stirring with a wooden spoon to mix well. Stir in nuts. Pour batter into the prepared pan.

Bake in a 350° oven about 20 minutes or till top springs back when touched lightly with finger. Cool in pan on a wire rack. Spread with Orange Icing. Cut into bars. Garnish bars with thin strips of orange peel, if desired. Makes 50.

ORANGE ICING: In a small bowl combine 2 cups sifted *powdered sugar*, 2 tablespoons *margarine* (softened), ½ teaspoon finely shredded *orange peel,* and 2 tablespoons *orange juice*; stir till smooth.

LEMON BARS

We reduced the margarine a bit and cut the cholesterol a little by substituting one egg white for a whole egg.

20% fewer calories

40% less fat

Per Cookie:

Calories	97
Total fat	3 g
Saturated fat	1 g
Cholesterol	13 mg
Sodium	41 mg
Carbohydrate	16 g
Fiber	<1 g
Protein	1 g

Nonstick spray coating
¾ cup all-purpose flour
3 tablespoons granulated sugar
¼ cup margarine
1 egg
1 egg white
⅔ cup granulated sugar
2 tablespoons all-purpose flour
¼ teaspoon finely shredded lemon peel
2 tablespoons lemon juice
1 tablespoon water
¼ teaspoon baking powder
1 tablespoon powdered sugar

Spray an 8x8x2-inch baking pan with nonstick coating; set pan aside.

In a small mixing bowl combine ¾ cup flour and 3 tablespoons granulated sugar. Cut in margarine till crumbly. Pat mixture onto the bottom of the prepared pan. Bake in a 350° oven for 15 minutes.

Meanwhile, in the same bowl combine egg and egg white. Beat with an electric mixer on medium speed till frothy. Add ⅔ cup granulated sugar, 2 tablespoons flour, lemon peel, lemon juice, water, and baking powder. Beat on medium speed for 3 minutes or till slightly thickened. Pour mixture over baked layer in pan. Bake for 20 to 25 minutes more or till edges are light brown and center is set. Cool in pan on a wire rack.

Sift powdered sugar over top. Cut into bars. Store in refrigerator. Makes 16.

STRAWBERRY SHORTBREAD

Sure to be a winner, we filled a reduced-fat shortbread with a low-sugar strawberry spread and glazed it with a lemony icing.

20% fewer calories

60% less fat

no cholesterol

45% less sodium

1¼ cups all-purpose flour
3 tablespoons sugar
¼ cup margarine
1 egg white
½ teaspoon finely shredded lemon peel

1 to 2 tablespoons water
¼ cup low-sugar strawberry spread
½ cup sifted powdered sugar
2 to 3 teaspoons lemon juice

Per Cookie:

Calories	99
Total fat	3 g
Saturated fat	1 g
Cholesterol	0 mg
Sodium	42 mg
Carbohydrate	16 g
Fiber	<1 g
Protein	1 g

In a medium mixing bowl stir together the flour and sugar. Cut in margarine till mixture resembles fine crumbs. Stir in egg white, lemon peel, and 1 tablespoon water. If dough is too crumbly, add an additional 1 tablespoon water. Form into a ball and knead till smooth. Divide dough in half. Shape each portion into an 8-inch log. Place the logs 4 to 5 inches apart on an ungreased cookie sheet. Pat each log into a 2-inch-wide strip. Using the back of a spoon, slightly press a 1-inch-wide indentation lengthwise down the center of each strip.

❧

Bake in a 325° oven for 20 to 25 minutes or until edges are light brown. Transfer cookie sheet to a wire rack. If necessary, re-shape the indentations in the shortbread by pressing with a spoon. Immediately spoon strawberry spread into the indentations. While shortbread is still warm, diagonally cut the strips crosswise into 1-inch-wide pieces. Cool.

❧

For icing, in a small bowl stir together powdered sugar and enough lemon juice to make an icing of drizzling consistency. Drizzle over bars. Makes 14.

PEANUT BUTTER-FRUIT SQUARES

These crispy no-bake cookies contain no cholesterol. For a change of pace, stir in snipped pitted prunes instead of mixed dried fruit.

Per Cookie:

Calories	83
Total Fat	3 g
Saturated fat	1 g
Cholesterol	0 mg
Sodium	70 mg
Carbohydrate	14 g
Fiber	< 1 g
Protein	2 g

¼ cup packed brown sugar
¼ cup light corn syrup
⅓ cup chunky peanut butter

2 cups crisp rice cereal
½ cup snipped mixed dried fruit

In a medium saucepan combine brown sugar and corn syrup. Cook and stir till mixture comes to boiling. Remove saucepan from heat. Stir in peanut butter till smooth. Stir in cereal and fruit.

❧

Press into an ungreased 8x8x2-inch baking pan. Cool on a wire rack till firm. Cut into squares. Makes 16.

ALMOND BISCOTTI

Biscotti are low-fat Italian biscuits that are baked first in a loaf, then sliced, and baked again. These extra-crunchy cookies are perfect for dipping into dessert wine or coffee.

50% fewer calories

60% less fat

Nonstick spray coating
¼ cup margarine, softened
½ cup sugar
1 teaspoon baking powder
2 eggs
½ teaspoon almond extract
2 cups all-purpose flour
⅓ cup chopped almonds, toasted

Per Cookie:

Calories	*42*
Total fat	*2 g*
Saturated fat	*<1 g*
Cholesterol	*9 mg*
Sodium	*14 mg*
Carbohydrate	*6 g*
Fiber	*<1 g*
Protein	*1 g*

Spray a cookie sheet with nonstick coating; set aside.

In a large mixing bowl, beat margarine with an electric mixer on medium to high speed for 30 seconds. Add sugar and baking powder; beat till well combined. Beat in eggs and almond extract. Mix well. Stir in flour with a wooden spoon, then stir in almonds.

On waxed paper, shape dough into two 12-inch-long logs. Place on prepared cookie sheet; flatten logs slightly to 1½-inch width. Bake in a 375° oven for 15 to 20 minutes or till firm and a wooden toothpick inserted in center comes out clean. Cool on wire rack. Cut each log into ½-inch slices, using a serrated knife.

Spray two cookie sheets with nonstick coating. On prepared cookie sheets, arrange slices, cut side down. Bake in a 300° oven for 10 minutes. Turn cookies over. Bake for 5 to 10 minutes more or till crisp and dry. Cool on wire racks. Makes 48.

PEPPERMINT STARS

Meringues are virtually fat-free and make good choices for dessert when you're watching your fat intake. They're fun to eat, too, because they melt like magic on your tongue.

Per Cookie:

Calories:	9
Total fat:	0 g
Saturated fat:	0 g
Cholesterol:	0 mg
Sodium:	2 mg
Carbohydrate:	2 g
Fiber:	0 g
Protein:	<1 g

2 egg whites
½ teaspoon vanilla
¼ teaspoon cream of tartar
½ cup sugar
¼ teaspoon peppermint extract
Red food coloring (optional)

Place egg whites in a medium mixing bowl; let stand at room temperature for 30 minutes.

Line two large cookie sheets with brown paper or foil; set aside.

Add vanilla and cream of tartar to egg whites. Beat with an electric mixer on medium to high speed till soft peaks form (tips curl). Gradually add sugar, *2 tablespoons* at a time, beating till stiff, glossy peaks form (tips stand straight) and sugar dissolves. Quickly beat in peppermint extract. Tint pink with several drops of red food coloring, if desired.

Using a pastry tube with a large star decorating tip, pipe cookies onto prepared cookie sheets (form cookies about 1½ inches in diameter). Bake in a 300° oven for 15 minutes. Turn off oven and let cookies dry in oven with door closed about 30 minutes. Remove from cookie sheets. Cover and store in a dry place. Makes 45.

DOUBLE CHOCOLATE DROPS

For a perfect snack, serve these rich morsels with hot cocoa (made from skim milk) and orange wedges.

Per Cookie:

Calories	*81*
Total fat	*3 g*
Saturated fat	*<1 g*
Cholesterol	*0 mg*
Sodium	*40 mg*
Carbohydrate	*14 g*
Fiber	*<1 g*
Protein	*1 g*

Nonstick spray coating
⅓ cup margarine, softened
¾ cup packed brown sugar
⅓ cup unsweetened cocoa powder
½ teaspoon baking powder
½ teaspoon baking soda
⅓ cup unsweetened applesauce
1 egg
1 teaspoon vanilla
1¾ cups all-purpose flour
½ cup miniature semisweet chocolate pieces
½ cup sifted powdered sugar
2 to 3 teaspoons skim milk

Spray a cookie sheet with nonstick coating; set cookie sheet aside.

In a large mixing bowl beat the margarine with an electric mixer on medium to high speed for 30 seconds. Add the brown sugar, cocoa powder, baking powder, and baking soda. Beat till thoroughly combined, scraping the sides of the bowl occasionally. Beat in the applesauce, egg, and vanilla. Beat in as much of the flour as you can with a mixer. Stir in any remaining flour with a wooden spoon. Stir in chocolate pieces. Drop dough by rounded teaspoons 2 inches apart on prepared cookie sheet.

Bake in a 375° oven for 8 to 10 minutes or till edges are light brown. Remove the cookies from the cookie sheet; cool on a wire rack. In a small bowl stir together the powdered sugar and milk. Drizzle over cookies. Store any leftover cookies in the freezer. Makes about 36.

CHEWY MOLASSES GINGER COOKIES

These cookies are every bit as hearty and spicy as their original counterparts, but the fat and the calories have been reduced.

30% fewer calories

65% less fat

Nonstick spray coating	1 egg
⅓ cup margarine, softened	¼ cup dark molasses
⅔ cup packed brown sugar	1½ cups all-purpose flour
1 teaspoon baking soda	½ cup whole wheat flour
1 teaspoon ground ginger	¼ cup granulated sugar
½ teaspoon ground cinnamon	1 teaspoon ground cinnamon

Per Cookie:

Calories	*50*
Total Fat	*1 g*
Saturated fat	*<1 g*
Cholesterol	*4 mg*
Sodium	*42 mg*
Carbohydrate	*9 g*
Fiber	*<1 g*
Protein	*1 g*

Spray cookie sheet with nonstick coating; set aside.

In a large mixing bowl beat the margarine with an electric mixer on medium to high speed for 30 seconds. Add the brown sugar, baking soda, ginger, and ½ teaspoon cinnamon; beat till combined. Beat in egg and molasses. Beat in as much of the all-purpose and whole wheat flour as you can with the mixer. Stir in any remaining flour with a wooden spoon. Cover and chill in the refrigerator for 1 hour.

Shape dough into 1-inch balls. Combine the granulated sugar and 1 teaspoon cinnamon. Roll balls in sugar-cinnamon mixture. Place 2 inches apart on prepared cookie sheet. Bake in a 350° oven for 10 to 11 minutes or till set and tops are cracked. Remove from cookie sheet. Cool on a wire rack. Makes about 4 dozen.

CHOCOLATE-PEANUT MERINGUE KISSES

To dress up these cookies for special occasions, sift a mixture of powdered sugar and cocoa powder over them.

50% fewer calories

Per Cookie:

Calories	*22*
Total Fat	*1 g*
Saturated fat	*<1 g*
Cholesterol	*0 mg*
Sodium	*4 mg*
Carbohydrate	*4 g*
Fiber	*<1 g*
Protein	*1 g*

2 egg whites
   Nonstick spray coating
½ teaspoon vanilla
½ cup sugar

2 tablespoons unsweetened
   cocoa powder
¼ cup finely chopped unsalted
   dry roasted peanuts

Place 2 egg whites in a small mixing bowl; let stand at room temperature for 30 minutes. Spray a cookie sheet with nonstick coating; set aside.

Add vanilla to egg whites. Beat with an electric mixer on medium to high speed about 1 minute or till soft peaks form (tips curl). Gradually add *¼ cup* of the sugar, *1 tablespoon* at a time, beating on high speed about 3 minutes more or till mixture forms stiff, glossy peaks (tips stand straight) and sugar dissolves. Stir together remaining sugar and cocoa powder; gently fold into beaten egg whites till well combined. (*Do not* overmix.) Fold in peanuts. Drop mixture by slightly rounded teaspoons onto prepared cookie sheet.

Bake in a 325° oven for 15 to 18 minutes or till light brown on bottoms. Remove from cookie sheet. Cool on a wire rack. Makes about 30.

APPLESAUCE-OATMEAL COOKIES WITH RAISINS

These soft, old-fashioned oatmeal cookies are dipped into a vanilla glaze for extra sweetness.

25% fewer calories

50% less fat

Nonstick spray coating
⅓ cup margarine, softened
¾ cup packed brown sugar
½ teaspoon ground cinnamon
¼ teaspoon baking soda
1 egg
½ cup unsweetened applesauce

1¼ cups all-purpose flour
1¼ cups regular or quick-cooking
  rolled oats
½ cup raisins
½ cup powdered sugar
1 teaspoon milk
¼ teaspoon vanilla

Per Cookie:

Calories	*88*
Total Fat	*3 g*
Saturated fat	*< 1 g*
Cholesterol	*7 mg*
Sodium	*35 mg*
Carbohydrate	*15 g*
Fiber	*< 1 g*
Protein	*1 g*

Spray a cookie sheet with nonstick coating; set cookie sheet aside.

In a large mixing bowl beat the margarine with an electric mixer on medium to high speed for 30 seconds. Add the brown sugar, cinnamon, and baking soda. Beat mixture till thoroughly combined, scraping the sides of the bowl occasionally. Beat in the egg and applesauce. Beat in as much of the flour as you can with the mixer. Stir in any remaining flour with a wooden spoon. Stir in the oats and raisins. Drop dough by rounded teaspoons 2 inches apart on prepared cookie sheet.

Bake in a 375° oven for 8 to 10 minutes or till edges are light brown. Remove cookies from cookie sheet. Cool on a wire rack.

For glaze, stir together powdered sugar, milk, and vanilla. Dip cooled cookies into glaze. Let dry on wire rack. Makes about 30.

CONFETTI OATMEAL DROPS

Freshly baked cookies like these soft, chewy oatmeals add a homemade goodness to any day of the week. Keep some in your freezer for surprise treats.

20% fewer calories

60% less fat

Per Cookie

Calories	70
Total Fat	2 g
Saturated fat:	<1 g
Cholesterol	7 mg
Sodium	26 mg
Carbohydrate	12 g
Fiber	<1 g
Protein	1 g

⅓ cup margarine, softened
⅔ cup sugar
1 teaspoon baking powder
1 teaspoon ground cinnamon
1 egg
½ cup finely shredded carrot
½ cup finely shredded zucchini
½ teaspoon vanilla
1½ cups all-purpose flour
¾ cup quick-cooking rolled oats
½ cup raisins

In a large mixing bowl beat the margarine with an electric mixer on medium to high speed for 30 seconds. Add the sugar, baking powder, and cinnamon. Beat mixture till thoroughly combined, scraping the sides of the bowl occasionally. Beat in the egg, carrot, zucchini, and vanilla. Beat in as much of the flour as you can with the mixer. Stir in any remaining flour, oats, and raisins with a wooden spoon. Drop dough by rounded teaspoons 2 inches apart onto ungreased cookie sheet.

❧

Bake in a 375° oven about 10 minutes or till golden. Remove cookies from cookie sheet. Cool on a wire rack. Makes about 32.

PIES, TARTS, AND PASTRIES

There's plenty of room for pies and tarts in your menu when you select one of these reduced-fat recipes. To help cut down on calories, all these desserts rely on a single crust, and we include two basic pastries for your use. In addition, you'll discover a crisp meringue crust, whole wheat pastry, and light, flaky phyllo crusts in the various recipes. For the fillings choose from glazed fresh strawberries, sliced melon, pink peppermint chiffon, and much, much more.

CHOCOLATE PIE

This chocolate pie has the creamy chocolate filling inside instead of under the meringue. The fat and calories from a conventional pie crust are missing.

55% fewer calories

95% less fat

95% less cholesterol

65% less sodium

3	egg whites	2½	cups skim milk
1	teaspoon vanilla	1½	teaspoons vanilla
¼	teaspoon cream of tartar	½	of an 8-ounce container
1	cup sugar		reduced fat frozen
½	cup sugar		whipped dessert topping,
¼	cup cornstarch		thawed (optional)
¼	cup unsweetened cocoa		Chocolate curls (optional)
	powder		Fresh mint leaves (optional)

Per Serving:

Calories	199
Total fat	1 g
Saturated fat	<1 g
Cholesterol	<1 mg
Sodium	61 mg
Carbohydrate	45 g
Fiber	<1 g
Protein	5 g

Cover a baking sheet with plain brown paper. Draw a 9-inch circle on paper; set aside.

For meringue shell "crust," in a mixing bowl combine egg whites, 1 teaspoon vanilla, and cream of tartar. Beat with an electric mixer on medium speed till soft peaks form (tips curl). Gradually add 1 cup sugar, *1 tablespoon* at a time, beating on high speed about 4 minutes more or till mixture forms stiff, glossy peaks (tips stand straight) and sugar dissolves. Pipe meringue through a pastry tube onto the circle on the brown paper, building up the sides to form a shell. Bake in a 300° oven for 45 minutes. Turn off oven and let dry in oven with door closed for 1 hour. Cool thoroughly on a wire rack.

Meanwhile, for filling, in a heavy saucepan combine ½ cup sugar, cornstarch, and cocoa powder. Stir in the milk. Cook and stir over medium heat till thickened and bubbly. Cook and stir 2 minutes more. Remove from heat. Stir in 1½ teaspoons vanilla. Cover surface with plastic wrap. Cool slightly without stirring, about 20 minutes. Pour into cooled meringue shell "crust." Cover and chill thoroughly. To serve, if desired, pipe or dollop whipped dessert topping atop filling and garnish with chocolate curls and mint sprigs. Makes 8 servings.

PINK PEPPERMINT CHIFFON PIE

Chiffons are traditionally lighter in texture but not necessarily in calories. We cut out fat and cholesterol by using whipped dessert topping and eliminating the egg yolks.

Per Serving:

Calories	207
Total fat	8 g
Saturated fat	1 g
Cholesterol	2 mg
Sodium	164 mg
Carbohydrate	35 g
Fiber	0 g
Protein	3 g

1 cup crushed chocolate wafers (16 wafers)
2 tablespoons margarine, melted
1 tablespoon sugar
3 cups tiny marshmallows
⅔ cup skim milk
½ teaspoon peppermint extract

4 drops red food coloring (optional)
2 egg whites (see tip, page 33)
3 tablespoons sugar
½ of an 8 ounce container reduced-fat frozen whipped dessert topping, thawed
Fresh mint leaves (optional)

For crumb crust, in a bowl stir together crushed wafers, margarine, and 1 tablespoon sugar with a fork. Press mixture into the bottom and up the sides of a 9-inch pie plate. Bake in a 375° oven for 5 minutes. Cool.

For filling, in medium saucepan combine marshmallows and milk. Cook and stir over medium heat till marshmallows are melted. Remove from heat. Stir in peppermint extract and red food coloring, if desired. Pour into a metal bowl. Chill till mixture begins to thicken, stirring occasionally.

Remove the peppermint mixture from the refrigerator (it will continue to set). In a medium mixing bowl immediately beat the egg whites with an electric mixer at medium speed till soft peaks form (tips curl). Gradually add the 3 tablespoons sugar, *1 tablespoon* at a time, beating on high speed till stiff peaks form (tips stand straight).

When peppermint mixture is partially set (consistency of unbeaten egg whites), fold in the egg white mixture. Fold in the thawed dessert topping. If necessary, chill the filling about 30 minutes or till it mounds when spooned. Spoon the filling into the crumb crust. Cover and chill for 4 to 24 hours or till set. If desired, garnish with additional dessert topping and mint leaves. Makes 8 servings.

25% fewer calories

50% less fat

55% less sodium

LIME CHIFFON PIE

If you're looking for an even lower-calorie dessert, try cutting this pie into 10 servings instead of 8. Each smaller serving is just 180 calories.

Per Serving:

Calories	225
Total fat	8 g
Saturated fat	2 g
Cholesterol	54 mg
Sodium	113 mg
Carbohydrate	32 g
Fiber	<1 g
Protein	5 g

Baked Pastry Shell (see recipe, page 174)
¼ cup sugar
1 envelope unflavored gelatin
½ cup water
1 teaspoon finely shredded lime peel (set aside)
¼ cup lime juice
2 egg yolks

3 drops green food coloring
3 egg whites (see tip, page 33)
¼ cup sugar
1 1.3-ounce envelope whipped dessert topping mix
½ cup skim milk
Whipped topping (optional)
Lime slices (optional)

Prepare Baked Pastry Shell as directed. Cool on a wire rack.

For filling, in a medium saucepan combine ¼ cup sugar and gelatin. Add water and lime juice. Cook and stir over low heat till gelatin is completely dissolved. Gradually stir all of the gelatin mixture into the egg yolks. Then return all of the egg yolk mixture to the saucepan. Bring to a gentle boil. Cook and stir for 2 minutes more. Remove from heat. Stir in lime peel and green food coloring. Cover and chill 30 minutes or till the consistency of corn syrup, stirring occasionally.

Remove the gelatin mixture from the refrigerator (it will continue to set). In a medium mixing bowl immediately beat the egg whites with an electric mixer on medium speed till soft peaks form (tips curl). Gradually add ¼ cup sugar, about *1 tablespoon* at a time, beating on high speed till stiff peaks form (tips stand straight). When gelatin is partially set (consistency of unbeaten egg whites), fold in the egg white mixture.

Wash the beaters and rinse with cold water. In a chilled bowl beat whipped dessert topping with milk according to package directions. Fold the whipped topping into the gelatin mixture. If necessary, chill the filling about 1 hour or till it mounds when spooned. Spoon the filling into the baked pie shell. Cover and chill for 4 to 24 hours or till set. If desired, garnish with additional whipped topping and lime slices. Makes 8 servings.

LEMON TART

We lightened the crust, reduced the sugar, and eliminated the egg yolks from a traditional lemon pie recipe. The reward: a tangy lemon tart at less than 170 calories per serving.

55% fewer calories

60% less cholesterol

35% less sodium

Pastry for Single-Crust Pie
(see recipe, page 174)
½ cup sugar
¼ cup cornstarch
1½ cups water
½ cup frozen egg product,
thawed

2 teaspoons finely shredded
lemon peel
¼ cup lemon juice
2 cups fresh blueberries, sliced
strawberries, and/or sliced
peeled peaches
Lemon slices (optional)

Per Serving:

Calories	*168*
Total fat	*5 g*
Saturated fat	*1 g*
Cholesterol	*0 mg*
Sodium	*76 mg*
Carbohydrate	*28 g*
Fiber	*1 g*
Protein	*3 g*

Prepare Pastry for Single-Crust Pie, *except* on a lightly floured surface, flatten the ball of dough with hands. Roll dough from center to the edges forming a circle about 13 inches in diameter. Ease pastry into an 11-inch tart pan with a removable bottom, being careful not to stretch the pastry. Trim even with edge of pan. Prick pastry generously with the tines of a fork. Bake in a 450° oven for 10 to 12 minutes or till golden. Cool on a wire rack.

❧

For filling, in a heavy medium saucepan stir together the sugar and cornstarch. Stir in the water. Cook and stir over medium-high heat till mixture is thickened and bubbly. Cook and stir for 2 minutes more. Remove from heat. Gradually stir about *1 cup* of the hot filling into the egg product. Return mixture to saucepan. Cook and stir till mixture almost comes to a boil; reduce heat, cook and stir for 2 minutes more. Remove from heat. Stir in the lemon peel and lemon juice. Spread into prepared tart shell. Cover and chill several hours. Before serving, remove sides of pan. Serve with fresh fruit. Garnish with lemon slices, if desired. Makes 10 servings.

BANANA CREAM PIE

Cutting the fat from favorite recipes is easy when you substitute reduced-fat ingredients and omit the margarine from the filling. That's what we did to lower fat and cut about 50 calories per serving from a traditional banana cream pie recipe.

45% less fat

95% less cholesterol

Per Serving:

Calories	313
Total fat	8 g
Saturated fat	2 g
Cholesterol	2 mg
Sodium	143 mg
Carbohydrate	54 g
Fiber	1 g
Protein	8 g

Baked Pastry Shell (see recipe, page 174)
2 tablespoons sugar
2 tablespoons unsweetened cocoa powder
½ cup sugar
½ cup all-purpose flour
3 cups skim milk
½ cup frozen egg product, thawed
2 teaspoons vanilla
2 medium bananas
1 tablespoon lemon juice
  Reduced-fat frozen whipped dessert topping, thawed
1 medium banana, sliced
¼ cup apricot or strawberry spreadable fruit, warmed
  Fresh mint leaves

Prepare Baked Pastry Shell as directed, *except* add 2 tablespoons sugar and cocoa powder with the flour when making the dough. Cool on a wire rack.

For filling, in a heavy saucepan combine ½ cup sugar and flour. Gradually stir in milk. Cook and stir over medium heat till mixture is thickened and bubbly. Cook and stir for 1 minute more. Remove from heat. Gradually stir about *1 cup* of the hot mixture into the egg product. Return all of the egg mixture to the saucepan. Bring almost to a boil. Cook and stir 2 minutes more. Remove from heat. Stir in vanilla.

Thinly slice the 2 bananas and arrange slices over bottom of crust. Pour the hot filling into crust. Cover and cool on wire rack till set. Cover and chill to store.

To serve, garnish pie around edge with dessert topping and 1 sliced banana. (Dip banana slices in lemon juice to prevent browning.) Drizzle with apricot spreadable fruit. Garnish with mint leaves. Makes 8 servings.

CRANBERRY-RASPBERRY TARTS

Frozen phyllo dough makes a fine crust because it bakes up so light and flaky without a lot of calories. Just before serving, lightly sift powdered sugar over the phyllo cups.

65% fewer calories

90% less fat

no cholesterol

80% less sodium

4 sheets frozen phyllo dough
     (17x12-inch rectangles),
     thawed
   Nonstick spray coating
½ cup packed brown sugar
1 tablespoon cornstarch

3 cups frozen unsweetened
     raspberries
2 cups cranberries
   Sifted powdered sugar
   Whipped topping or Whipped
     Milk Topping (see recipes,
     page 9) (optional)

Per Serving:

Calories	114
Total fat	1 g
Saturated fat	<1 g
Cholesterol	0 mg
Sodium	50 mg
Carbohydrate	25 g
Fiber	3 g
Protein	1 g

Grease six 6-ounce custard cups; set aside. Unfold phyllo dough. Place *one sheet* of phyllo dough on a cutting board. Spray with nonstick coating. Repeat layering and spraying remaining phyllo, keeping phyllo covered with a damp cloth and removing only one sheet at a time.

Using a sharp knife, cut the phyllo stack lengthwise into 6 strips. Then cut the strips crosswise into thirds forming 18 rectangles. Carefully press 3 rectangles into each prepared custard cup so that the entire cup is covered with phyllo. Set the phyllo-lined custard cups on a baking sheet.

Meanwhile, in a large saucepan combine brown sugar and cornstarch; add raspberries and cranberries. Cook and stir over medium heat till thickened and bubbly. Pour the cranberry mixture into phyllo-lined custard cups.

Bake in a 350° oven for 25 to 30 minutes or till phyllo is golden. Cool completely on a wire rack. Sift powdered sugar lightly over phyllo cups or serve with dollops of whipped topping, if desired. Makes 8 servings.

GLAZED STRAWBERRY PIE

Fresh whole strawberries are folded into an easy-to-make fresh strawberry sauce and then turned into a lightened oil pie crust. Simply luscious with or without the whipped topping.

30% fewer calories

Baked Oil Pastry Shell
   (see recipe, page 175)
6 cups strawberries, hulled
1 cup water
¼ cup sugar
2 tablespoons cornstarch

Red food coloring
Thin strips of orange peel
  (optional)
Whipped Topping or Whipped
  Milk Topping (see recipes,
  page 9) (optional)

Per Serving:

Calories	178
Total fat	6 g
Saturated fat	1 g
Cholesterol	<1 mg
Sodium	78 mg
Carbohydrate	30 g
Fiber	3 g
Protein	3 g

Prepare Baked Oil Pastry Shell as directed. Cool on a wire rack.

In food processor bowl or blender container, place *1 cup* of the strawberries and water. Cover and process or blend till smooth. Transfer to a small saucepan. Bring to boiling; simmer 2 minutes.

In 2- or 3-quart saucepan stir together sugar and cornstarch. Stir in berry mixture. Cook and stir over medium heat till mixture is thickened and bubbly. Cook and stir for 2 minutes more. Remove from heat. Stir in enough red food coloring to tint a rich red color. Cool to room temperature.

Fold remaining strawberries into cooled mixture. Turn into baked pie shell. Cover and chill 3 to 4 hours.

If desired, garnish with thin strips of orange peel or serve with dollops of whipped topping. Makes 8 servings.

BLUEBERRY CHEESE PIE

Fresh or frozen blueberries make an elegant crown for this lemon-flavored cheese pie. The fat-free cream cheese makes a fine substitute for regular cream cheese.

45% fewer calories

70% less fat

Per Serving:

Calories _____ 197
Total fat _____ 5 g
  Saturated fat _____ 1 g
Cholesterol _____ 4 mg
Sodium _____ 221 mg
Carbohydrate _____ 32 g
Fiber _____ 2 g
Protein _____ 7 g

Baked Pastry Shell (see recipe, page 174)
1 8-ounce container fat-free cream cheese product
1 teaspoon finely shredded lemon peel
1 tablespoon lemon juice
4 cups fresh or frozen blueberries, thawed
½ cup sugar
2 tablespoons cornstarch
1 tablespoon lemon juice

Prepare Baked Pastry Shell as directed. Cool on a wire rack.

For filling, in a medium mixing bowl combine cream cheese product, lemon peel, and 1 tablespoon lemon juice. Stir till smooth. Spread filling in baked shell. Sprinkle *2 cups* of the blueberries over filling. Cover and chill.

For sauce, in a shallow dish mash remaining blueberries with a fork. In a 2-cup measure, place blueberries. Add enough water to make 1½ cups. In a heavy medium saucepan combine sugar and cornstarch. Stir in blueberry mixture. Cook and stir over medium heat till mixture is thickened and bubbly. Cook and stir for 2 minutes more. Remove from heat; stir in 1 tablespoon lemon juice. Cool to lukewarm.

Spoon blueberry sauce over blueberries in pastry shell. Cover and chill for 3 hours or till set. Makes 10 servings.

STRAWBERRY-RHUBARB PIE

Pie crusts are traditionally high in fat and calories. This recipe turns out a flavorful pie crust made with oil and egg white. By using only one crust and a crumbly topper, you save calories and fat.

40% fewer calories

60% less fat

no cholesterol

75% less sodium

Nonstick spray coating
1 cup all-purpose flour
1 teaspoon baking powder
1 egg white, beaten
2 tablespoons cooking oil
2 tablespoons skim milk
½ cup sugar

¼ cup all-purpose flour
2 cups diced rhubarb
2 cups sliced strawberries
⅓ cup all-purpose flour
⅓ cup sugar
1 teaspoon ground cinnamon
2 tablespoons margarine, melted

Per Serving:

Calories	242
Total fat	7 g
Saturated fat	1 g
Cholesterol	0 mg
Sodium	47 mg
Carbohydrate	43 g
Fiber	2 g
Protein	3 g

Spray a 9-inch pie plate with nonstick coating; set pie plate aside.

For pastry, in a medium mixing bowl stir together 1 cup flour and baking powder. Stir together egg white, oil, and milk. Add egg mixture to flour mixture. Gently toss with a fork till mixture is moistened. Form into a ball.

On a lightly floured surface, flatten the ball of dough with hands. Roll dough from center to the edges forming a circle about 11 inches in diameter. Ease pastry into prepared pie plate, being careful not to stretch pastry. Trim the pastry to ½ inch beyond the edge of the pie plate. Fold under the extra pastry and flute the edge high.

In a large mixing bowl stir together ½ cup sugar and ¼ cup flour. Add rhubarb and strawberries. Toss to mix. Transfer mixture to pie shell. In a small mixing bowl combine ⅓ cup flour, ⅓ cup sugar, cinnamon, and melted margarine. Mix till crumbly. Sprinkle over rhubarb mixture.

Bake in a 350° oven for 50 minutes or till rhubarb is tender when tested with a wooden toothpick. Cool on a wire rack. Makes 8 servings.

SUMMER FRUIT TART

One look at the photo will convince you this is quite an impressive dessert. It tastes as good as it looks, too, and has less than 200 calories per serving. We saved calories and fat by using a lighter crust without ground nuts.

Per Serving:

Calories	187
Total fat	6 g
Saturated fat	1 g
Cholesterol	1 mg
Sodium	84 mg
Carbohydrate	31 g
Fiber	2 g
Protein	4 g

Pastry for a Single-Crust Pie
  (see recipe, page 174)
¼ cup sugar
2 tablespoons cornstarch
1 12-ounce can evaporated skim
   milk
¼ cup frozen egg product,
   thawed

½ teaspoon vanilla
2 medium peeled peaches or
   nectarines, thinly sliced
2 plums, thinly sliced
2 kiwi fruit, peeled and sliced
¼ cup blueberries or blackberries
2 tablespoons honey
1 tablespoon rum or orange
   juice

Prepare Pastry for a Single-Crust Pie, *except* on a lightly floured surface, flatten the ball of dough with hands. Roll dough from center to the edges forming a circle about 13 inches in diameter. Ease pastry into an 11-inch tart pan with removable bottom, being careful not to stretch the pastry. Trim even with edge of pan. Prick pastry generously with the tines of a fork. Bake in a 450° oven for 10 to 12 minutes or till golden. Cool on a wire rack.

For filling, in a heavy medium saucepan stir together the sugar and cornstarch; stir in the evaporated skim milk and egg product. Cook and stir over medium heat till mixture is thickened and bubbly. Cook and stir for 2 minutes more. Remove from the heat. Stir in vanilla. Cover surface with plastic wrap and chill thoroughly.

Spread cooled filling in baked tart shell. Arrange peaches, plums, and kiwi in concentric circles atop filling. Add berries to the center and randomly sprinkle any extra berries over the top. In a small bowl combine honey and rum or orange juice. Brush fruit with honey mixture. Cover and chill up to 1 hour. Before serving, remove sides of pan. Makes 10 servings.

STRAWBERRY-ORANGE TART

For a flavor boost, stir 1 teaspoon finely-shredded orange peel into the pastry dough and then roll out as usual.

40% fewer calories

40% less fat

65% less cholesterol

Pastry for a Single-Crust Pie
(see recipe, page 174)
1　8-ounce package reduced-fat
cream cheese (Neufchâtel),
softened
¼　cup sugar
1　teaspoon finely shredded
orange peel
1　tablespoon orange juice

⅔　cup orange juice
1　tablespoon sugar
2　teaspoons cornstarch
2　oranges, peeled and sectioned
1　pint strawberries, hulled and
halved
Thin strips of orange peel
(optional)
Thin strips of lime peel
(optional)

Per Serving:

Calories	*206*
Total fat	*11 g*
Saturated fat	*5 g*
Cholesterol	*18 mg*
Sodium	*149 mg*
Carbohydrate	*24 g*
Fiber	*1 g*
Protein	*4 g*

Prepare Pastry for a Single-Crust Pie, *except* on a lightly floured surface, flatten the ball of dough with hands. Roll dough from center to the edges forming a circle about 13 inches in diameter. Ease pastry into an 11-inch tart pan with removable bottom, being careful not to stretch the pastry. Trim even with edge of pan. Prick pastry generously with the tines of a fork. Bake in a 450° oven for 10 to 12 minutes or till golden. Cool on a wire rack.

For filling, in a medium mixing bowl combine reduced-fat cream cheese, ¼ cup sugar, 1 teaspoon orange peel, and 1 tablespoon orange juice. Beat with an electric mixer on high speed till light and fluffy. Spread cheese filling in baked tart shell.

For glaze, in a small saucepan combine ⅔ cup orange juice, 1 tablespoon sugar, and cornstarch. Cook and stir over medium heat till mixture is thickened and bubbly. Cook and stir for 2 minutes more. Remove from the heat. Cool thoroughly.

Arrange orange sections and strawberry halves atop cheese filling. Spoon orange glaze over all. Sprinkle with thin strips of orange peel and lime peel, if desired. Cover and chill 6 hours or till serving time. Makes 10 servings.

RASPBERRY TARTLETS

The filling is light because it includes nonfat ricotta cheese and plain nonfat yogurt instead of regular cream cheese.

Per Serving:

Calories _____ 231
Total fat _____ 9 g
  Saturated fat _____ 1 g
Cholesterol _____ 2 mg
Sodium _____ 63 mg
Carbohydrate _____ 31 g
Fiber _____ 2 g
Protein _____ 7 g

1⅔ cups all-purpose flour
2 tablespoons sugar
⅛ teaspoon salt
⅓ cup cooking oil
3 to 4 tablespoons water
3 tablespoons sugar
1½ teaspoons unflavored gelatin
¼ cup water
1 8-ounce carton plain nonfat yogurt

¾ cup nonfat ricotta cheese
1 teaspoon vanilla
½ teaspoon finely shredded orange peel
1 cup raspberries or Raspberry Sauce (see recipe, page 12)
Orange peel curls (optional)
Fresh mint leaves (optional)

For crust, in a medium mixing bowl stir together flour, 2 tablespoons sugar, and salt. Gradually add the oil, stirring quickly with a fork till mixture resembles fine crumbs. Sprinkle *1 tablespoon* of the water over part of the mixture; gently toss with a fork. Push moistened dough to the side of the bowl. Repeat, using 1 tablespoon of the remaining water at a time, till all dough is moistened.

On a lightly floured surface, roll dough to slightly less than ⅛-inch thick. Cut into eight 5-inch circles. (Reroll dough as necessary.) Place dough into eight 3½-inch tart pans. Flute edges. Prick bottoms and sides of dough generously with tines of a fork. Bake in a 400° oven for 12 to 15 minutes or till golden. Cool on wire rack; remove from pans.

For filling, in a small saucepan stir together 3 tablespoons sugar and gelatin. Add ¼ cup water. Cook and stir over low heat till sugar and gelatin are dissolved. Cool. In a blender container or food processor bowl combine the yogurt, ricotta cheese, vanilla, orange peel, and gelatin mixture. Cover and blend or process till smooth. Cover; chill in refrigerator till mixture mounds when spooned, stirring occasionally (about 1 hour).

Spoon ricotta mixture into baked tart shells; cover and chill about 30 minutes. Top with raspberries or Raspberry Sauce just before serving. Garnish with orange peel curls and mint leaves, if desired. Makes 8 servings.

ASSORTED FRUIT TART

This light-style tart features a cookielike crust that's a snap to prepare. Just press the dough into the pan before baking—no rolling and no mess.

Per Serving:

Calories	157
Total Fat	4 g
Saturated fat	1 g
Cholesterol	1 mg
Sodium	56 mg
Carbohydrate	25 g
Fiber	1 g
Protein	4 g

Nonstick spray coating
¼ cup margarine, softened
⅓ cup granulated sugar
1 teaspoon finely shredded lemon peel
1 egg white
½ teaspoon vanilla
1¼ cups all-purpose flour
⅔ cup nonfat ricotta cheese
1 tablespoon powdered sugar

¼ teaspoon vanilla
2 cups sliced strawberries
1 medium peach, peeled, pitted, and thinly sliced
1 medium plum, pitted and thinly sliced
1 cup halved seedless green grapes
¼ cup lower sugar apricot spread
1 tablespoon water

Spray a 12-inch tart or pizza pan with nonstick coating; set pan aside.

In a medium mixing bowl beat margarine with an electric mixer on medium to high speed for 30 seconds. Add the ⅓ cup granulated sugar and lemon peel; beat till combined. Beat in the egg white and ½ teaspoon vanilla till combined. Beat in as much of the flour as you can with the mixer. Stir in any remaining flour with a wooden spoon. Press mixture into the prepared pan.

Bake in a 350° oven for 12 to 15 minutes or till edges are lightly browned. Cool completely on wire rack.

Meanwhile, in a small mixing bowl combine ricotta cheese, powdered sugar, and ¼ teaspoon vanilla. Spread on cooled crust. Arrange strawberries, peaches, plums, and grapes on top. In a small saucepan combine apricot spread and water; stir over low heat till spread melts. Brush fruit with apricot mixture. Chill in the refrigerator up to 2 hours or till serving time. To serve, cut into thin wedges. Makes 12 servings.

Minted Melon Tart
With Blueberries

Honeydew melon can be substituted for half of the cantaloupe in this recipe. Just alternate the melon slices over the crust before spooning the apple juice glaze over all.

1   cup crushed graham crackers
3   tablespoons margarine, melted
1   tablespoon sugar
½   cup frozen apple juice
       concentrate
½   cup water

1   tablespoon cornstarch
1   tablespoon lemon juice
1   sprig fresh mint
1   cantaloupe, seeded, peeled,
       and cut into thin slices
½   cup fresh blueberries
       Fresh mint leaves (optional)

Per Serving:

Calories	179
Total Fat	5 g
Saturated fat	1 g
Cholesterol	0 mg
Sodium	144 mg
Carbohydrate	32 g
Fiber	3 g
Protein	2 g

For crust, in a small mixing bowl combine the crushed graham crackers, melted margarine, and sugar. Press the mixture onto the bottom of a 10-inch springform pan. Bake in a 350° oven for 10 minutes. Cool in pan on a wire rack.

For glaze, in a small saucepan combine the apple juice concentrate, water, cornstarch, lemon juice, and 1 sprig of mint. Cook and stir mixture till thickened and bubbly. Cook and stir for 2 minutes more. Remove from heat. Remove mint.

Arrange melon slices in cooled crust by overlapping slices in concentric circles from outer edge to center. Top with blueberries. Drizzle with glaze. Cover and chill for 2 to 4 hours. If desired, garnish with mint leaves. Makes 8 servings.

PEACH TART WITH WHOLE WHEAT PASTRY

Take advantage of fresh summer peaches in this crumb-topped tart and add a homespun dessert to your menu. The whole wheat flour adds a nutty taste to the crust.

45% fewer calories

60% less fat

no cholesterol

50% less sodium

¾ cup all-purpose flour
½ cup whole wheat flour
¼ cup margarine
3 to 4 tablespoons cold water
⅓ cup sugar
2 tablespoons all-purpose flour
½ teaspoon ground nutmeg

6 cups sliced, peeled pitted peaches
⅓ cup toasted wheat germ
2 tablespoons all-purpose flour
2 tablespoons brown sugar
2 tablespoons margarine, melted
1 teaspoon ground cinnamon

Per Serving:

Calories	218
Total fat	8 g
Saturated fat	1 g
Cholesterol	0 mg
Sodium	82 mg
Carbohydrate	36 g
Fiber	3 g
Protein	4 g

In a medium mixing bowl stir together the ¾ cup all-purpose flour and the whole wheat flour. Using a pastry blender, cut in ¼ cup margarine till mixture resembles fine crumbs. Sprinkle *1 tablespoon* of the water over part of the mixture; gently toss with a fork. Push moistened dough to the side of the bowl. Repeat, using 1 tablespoon of the remaining water at a time, till all the dough is moistened. Form dough into a ball.

On a lightly floured surface, flatten the ball of dough with hands. Roll dough from center to the edges forming a circle about 13 inches in diameter. Ease pastry into an 11-inch tart pan with a removable bottom, being careful not to stretch the pastry. Trim even with edge of pan. Line pastry with a double thickness of foil. Bake in a 450° oven for 8 minutes. Remove foil. Bake for 4 to 5 minutes more or till set and dry.

In a large bowl combine ⅓ cup sugar, 2 tablespoons all-purpose flour, and nutmeg. Add peach slices, tossing to coat. Turn peach mixture into crust. In a medium bowl stir together the wheat germ, 2 tablespoons all-purpose flour, brown sugar, 2 tablespoons melted margarine, and the cinnamon. Sprinkle crumb topping evenly over peaches. Bake in a 375° oven about 45 minutes or till crust is golden and filling is bubbly. Serve warm or cool. Makes 10 servings.

UPSIDE-DOWN CARAMELIZED APPLE PIE

Here's a lightened version of the classic French tarte tatin—an upside-down apple tart with a luscious caramel glaze. It's best if served warm from the oven.

Per Serving:

Calories	289
Total Fat	13 g
Saturated fat	3 g
Cholesterol	0 mg
Sodium	140 mg
Carbohydrate	44 g
Fiber	2 g
Protein	2 g

Pastry for Single-Crust Pie (see recipe, page 174)
⅓ cup sugar
4 teaspoons cornstarch
1 teaspoon ground cinnamon
1 teaspoon finely shredded lemon peel
1 tablespoon lemon juice
¼ teaspoon ground ginger
6 to 8 apples, peeled, cored, and sliced (6 cups)
¼ cup margarine
⅓ cup sugar

Prepare Pastry for Single-Crust Pie, *except* roll dough between 2 pieces of waxed paper forming a circle about 10 inches in diameter; set aside.

❧

For filling, in large bowl stir together ⅓ cup sugar, cornstarch, cinnamon, lemon peel, lemon juice, and ginger; add apple slices. Toss till apples are coated. Set aside.

❧

In 10-inch oven-going* skillet melt margarine. Add remaining ⅓ cup sugar and cook till mixture is golden, stirring frequently. Remove from heat. Arrange apple slices in skillet. Remove waxed paper from pastry. Place pastry atop apples. Cut slits in top of pastry.

❧

Bake in a 400° oven for 30 to 35 minutes or till crust is golden. Cool on wire rack for 10 minutes. Using a knife, loosen sides of crust from skillet, if necessary. Invert onto serving plate. If some of the apples stick to the skillet, lift them off with a spatula and rearrange them on top of the pie. Spoon any remaining syrup over apples. Serve warm. Makes 8 servings.

❧

*To make skillet oven-going, cover handle with aluminum foil.

PASTRY FOR SINGLE-CRUST PIE

We've reduced the shortening slightly in this lighter pie crust without sacrificing its flaky nature. Remember a gram of fat saved here and there really adds up.

Per Serving
(⅛ of pastry):

Calories	*122*
Total fat	*7 g*
Saturated fat	*2 g*
Cholesterol	*0 g*
Sodium	*67 mg*
Carbohydrate	*14 g*
Fiber	*<1 g*
Protein	*2 g*

1¼ cups all-purpose flour
¼   teaspoon salt

¼   cup shortening
4   to 5 tablespoons cold water

In a medium mixing bowl stir together the flour and salt. Using a pastry blender, cut in shortening till mixture resembles fine crumbs. Sprinkle *1 tablespoon* of the water over part of the mixture; gently toss with a fork. Push moistened dough to the side of the bowl. Repeat, using 1 tablespoon of the remaining water at a time, till all dough is moistened. Form dough into a ball.

On a lightly floured surface, flatten the ball of dough with hands. Roll dough from center to the edges forming a circle about 12 inches in diameter. Ease pastry into a 9-inch pie plate, being careful not to stretch pastry.

Trim the pastry to ½ inch beyond the edge of the pie plate. Fold under the extra pastry and flute the edge. Do not prick pastry. Bake as directed in individual recipes.

BAKED PASTRY SHELL: Prepare Pastry for Single-Crust Pie as above, *except* prick bottom and sides of pastry generously with the tines of a fork. Also prick where bottom and sides meet all around pie shell. Bake in a 450° oven for 12 to 15 minutes or till golden. Cool pie crust on a wire rack. Fill as directed in individual recipes.

OIL PASTRY FOR SINGLE-CRUST PIE

Save a couple of grams of fat per serving by preparing this pastry for your pies. Use it in any of the pie recipes calling for a Baked Pastry Shell.

1¼   cups all-purpose flour
¼   teaspoon salt

¼   cup skim milk
3   tablespoons cooking oil

Per serving
(⅛ of pastry):

Calories_____113
Total fat_____5 g
  Saturated fat_____1 g
Cholesterol_____<1 mg
Sodium_____71 mg
Carbohydrate_____14 g
Fiber_____<1 g
Protein_____2 g

In a medium mixing bowl stir together the flour and salt. In a 1-cup measure combine milk and oil. Add oil mixture all at once to flour mixture. Stir with a fork till dough fork till dough forms

❧

On a lightly floured surface, flatten the ball of dough with hands. Roll dough from center to the edges forming a circle about 12 inches in diameter. Ease pastry into a 9-inch pie plate, being careful not to stretch the pastry.

❧

Trim the pastry to ½ inch beyond the edge of the pie plate. Fold under the extra pastry and flute the edge. Do not prick pastry. Bake as directed in individual recipes.

BAKED OIL PASTRY SHELL: Prepare Oil Pastry for Single-Crust Pie as above, *except* prick bottom and sides of pastry generously with the tines of a fork. Also prick where bottom and sides meet all around pie shell. Bake in a 450° oven for 10 to 12 minutes or till crust is golden. Cool pie crust on a wire rack. Fill as directed in individual recipes.

GLAZED FRUIT TURNOVERS

Phyllo is substituted for the pastry typically used to make turnovers.

Per Serving:

Calories	120
Total fat	2 g
Saturated fat	<1 g
Cholesterol	<1 g
Sodium	71 mg
Carbohydrate	26 g
Fiber	1 g
Protein	1 g

1 cup chopped, peeled apple or pear
2 tablespoons raisins or snipped apricots
1 tablespoon granulated sugar
1 teaspoon all-purpose flour
1 teaspoon lemon juice
½ teaspoon ground cinnamon
Dash ground nutmeg
3 sheets frozen phyllo dough (17x12-inch rectangles), thawed
Nonstick spray coating
¼ cup sifted powdered sugar
1 teaspoon skim milk

For filling, in a small mixing bowl combine apple or pear, raisins or apricots, granulated sugar, flour, lemon juice, cinnamon, and nutmeg. Set aside. Unfold phyllo dough. Place *one sheet* of phyllo dough on a cutting board. Spray with nonstick coating. Repeat layering and spraying remaining phyllo, keeping phyllo covered with a damp cloth, and removing only one sheet at a time. Using a sharp knife, cut the stack lengthwise into 4 strips.

For each turnover, spoon about *one-fourth* of the filling about 1 inch from the end of *each* strip. Fold the end over the filling at a 45 angle. Continue folding to form a triangle that encloses the filling, using the entire strip. Repeat with remaining strips of phyllo and filling. Spray tops with nonstick coating.

Spray a baking sheet with nonstick coating. Place triangles on the baking sheet. Bake in a 350° oven about 15 minutes or till golden.

For glaze, in a small bowl combine powdered sugar and milk. Drizzle over warm turnovers. Serve warm or cool. Makes 4 servings.

FROZEN DESSERTS

*T*he next best thing to fresh fruit is its frozen, concentrated flavor as in the Gingered Pear Sorbet Dessert or Fresh Lime Sorbet. There's a rainbow of other homemade choices running from a coffee granita to Creamy Pineapple Sherbet. Or freeze a special pie combination, a dozen tortoni cups, or eight strawberry bombes. All of these make-ahead desserts store well and are light, refreshing endings to a meal. To calculate the savings in calories and fat, for most of the sorbet, sherbet, ice milk, and frozen yogurt recipes, we compared them to recipes with ice cream.

FRESH LIME SORBET

Since the flavorings in this sorbet are reminiscent of frozen rum daiquiris, why not serve up small scoops of this refreshing sorbet in stemmed glasses and garnish with a lime twist? (The sorbet saves calories compared with lime sherbet.)

40% fewer calories

no fat

no cholesterol

3 cups water
1 cup sugar
1 teaspoon finely shredded
      lime peel

½ cup fresh lime juice
2 tablespoons light rum
      Few drops green food coloring

Per Serving:

Calories	*96*
Total Fat	*0 g*
Saturated fat	*0 g*
Cholesterol	*0 mg*
Sodium	*3 mg*
Carbohydrate	*23 g*
Fiber	*0 g*
Protein	*0 g*

In a medium saucepan combine the water and sugar. Bring to boiling; remove from heat. Cool thoroughly. Cover and chill.

In a 9x9x2-inch baking pan combine the chilled syrup mixture, lime peel, lime juice, and rum. Add food coloring. Cover and freeze about 3 to 4 hours or till almost firm.

Break the frozen mixture into small chunks. Transfer chunks to a chilled mixing bowl. Beat with an electric mixer on medium speed till fluffy but not melted. Return quickly to the chilled pan. Cover and freeze till firm.

To serve, let stand at room temperature for 5 minutes before serving. Makes about 4½ cups or 9 servings.

STRAWBERRY DAIQUIRI SORBET

For fun, serve this sorbet in stemmed glasses with sugared rims. Just moisten the edge of each glass with lime juice and dip into sugar. Garnish with a lime slice and a whole strawberry.

Per Serving:

Calories	78
Total fat	<1 g
Saturated fat	1 g
Cholesterol	0 mg
Sodium	2 mg
Carbohydrate	18 g
Fiber	2 g
Protein	<1 g

1½	cups water	2	teaspoons finely shredded lime peel
1	cup sugar	¼	cup lime juice
8	cups strawberries, hulled	1	tablespoon orange liqueur
¼	cup light rum		Lime peel twists (optional)

In a medium saucepan, combine water and sugar. Cook and stir over high heat till mixture comes to a boil and sugar dissolves. Remove from heat and cool syrup completely.

Place strawberries in a food processor bowl or blender container. Cover and process or blend till nearly smooth. (For best results, puree half at a time.) In a bowl stir together pureed strawberries, rum, lime peel, lime juice, and orange liqueur. Stir in cooled syrup.

Freeze the mixture in a 4-quart ice cream freezer according to the manufacturer's directions. Using a small ice cream scoop, scoop sorbet into dishes. Garnish with lime peel twists, if desired. Makes 2 quarts or 16 servings.

PINK GRAPEFRUIT SORBET

This pale pink sorbet has a mild, delightful flavor. It's great served by itself or on top of fruit salad or compote.

85% less fat

no cholesterol

Per Serving:

Calories	144
Total fat	<1 g
Saturated fat	<1 g
Cholesterol	0 mg
Sodium	2 mg
Carbohydrate	36 g
Fiber	<1 g
Protein	1 g

6 pink or white grapefruit
1 cup sugar

1 tablespoon lemon juice
1 tablespoon Campari (optional)

Using a vegetable peeler, remove the zest (colored part) from the peel of 1 grapefruit. Coarsely chop the zest. In a food processor bowl or blender container, place chopped zest and sugar. Cover and process or blend till zest is very finely chopped.

Squeeze enough juice from the grapefruit to make 4 cups juice. Add zest mixture, lemon juice, and Campari, if desired. Mix well.

Freeze the mixture in a 4-quart ice cream freezer according to manufacturer's directions. Makes 1 quart or 8 servings.

MELON SORBET

For a delightful combination, prepare both cantaloupe and honeydew sorbet. Serve in dessert dishes using a melon baller or a small ice cream scoop. Garnish with slivered lime peel.

6   cups cantaloupe or honeydew
      melon cubes (1-inch cubes)
½   cup light corn syrup

2   teaspoons finely shredded
      lemon peel
¼   cup lemon juice

In a blender container or food processor bowl blend or process melon cubes, half at a time, until pureed. Combine pureed melon, corn syrup, lemon peel, and lemon juice. Freeze the mixture in a 1- or 2-quart ice cream freezer according to the manufacturer's directions. Makes about 1 quart or 8 servings.

Per Serving:

Calories	*104*
Total fat	*<1 g*
Saturated fat	*0 g*
Cholesterol	*0 mg*
Sodium	*26 mg*
Carbohydrate	*26 g*
Fiber	*1 g*
Protein	*1 g*

CHOCOLATE ALMOND COFFEE GRANITA

For the garnish, prepare the cookie batter in the recipe for Chocolate Sundaes in Cookie Cups on page 192. Bake as directed and shape by rolling warm cookies into cylinders instead of draping over custard cups.

2	cups water	2	teaspoons instant coffee crystals
½	cup sugar		Several drops almond extract
1	tablespoon unsweetened cocoa powder		

In a small bowl combine the water, sugar, cocoa powder, coffee crystals, and almond extract. Stir till sugar and cocoa are dissolved. Pour the mixture into an 8x4x2-inch or a 9x5x3-inch loaf pan. Cover and freeze, about 6 hours or till solid.

❧

With a large spoon or fork, break the frozen mixture into coarse ice crystals. Return to freezer for 1 to 2 hours more. Stir again, working quickly to break granita into finer ice crystals. This step may be repeated at 30-minute intervals until desired consistency is reached or freeze overnight.

❧

Spoon into individual dessert glasses. Serve immediately. Makes about 2 cups or 4 servings.

Per Serving:

Calories	98
Total Fat	<1 g
Saturated fat	0 g
Cholesterol	0 mg
Sodium	4 mg
Carbohydrate	25 g
Fiber	0 g
Protein	<1 g

EXTRA-LIGHT

ORANGE ICE IN ORANGE CUPS

This frosty-smooth orange ice concentrates the refreshing flavor of the orange. It's practically fat-free and so attractive with a sprig of fresh mint.

1   orange
1   cup water
⅔   cup sugar
1½ cups orange juice
2   tablespoons lemon juice

6   Orange Cups (optional) or
    ¾ cup Raspberry Sauce
    (see recipe, page 12)
    Fresh mint leaves

Using a vegetable peeler, remove the zest (colored part) from the orange peel.

In a small saucepan combine orange zest, water, and sugar. Bring to boiling, stirring till sugar dissolves. Reduce heat; simmer, covered, for 5 minutes. Strain; cool. Add orange juice and lemon juice. Pour orange juice mixture into a 8x4x2-inch loaf pan. Cover and freeze till firm.

To serve, break frozen mixture into chunks. Place in a metal mixing bowl. Beat with an electric mixer till mixture is slushy. (Slushy mixture may be refrozen.) Spoon into Orange Cups, if desired, or spoon into dishes and serve with Raspberry Sauce. Garnish with mint leaves. Makes 3 cups or 6 servings.

ORANGE CUPS: Cut 3 *oranges* into halves. Scoop out orange pulp with a grapefruit knife or a spoon and save for another use. Using a knife or scissors, cut a saw-toothed or scalloped edge around each orange half.

FROZEN BANANA SPLIT PIE

Now you can freeze a lightened version of this soda fountain favorite in your own freezer.

40% fewer calories

75% less fat

Per Serving:

Calories_____225
Total fat_____5 g
  Saturated fat_____1 g
Cholesterol_____2 mg
Sodium_____206 mg
Carbohydrate_____42 g
Fiber_____<1 g
Protein_____7 g

1 cup crushed chocolate wafers (19 wafers)
2 tablespoons margarine, melted
1 pint vanilla fat-free frozen dessert or ice milk, softened
1 pint strawberry fat-free frozen dessert or ice milk, softened
1 medium banana, thinly sliced
½ cup Chocolate Dessert Sauce (see recipe, page 10)

For crumb crust, in a small bowl stir together crushed wafers and melted margarine. Press mixture onto the bottom and up the sides of a 9-inch pie plate. Bake in a 375° oven for 5 minutes. Cool completely on a wire rack.

❧

Carefully spread the vanilla frozen dessert or ice milk in the bottom of cooled chocolate crust. Cover and freeze till firm. Top with a layer of strawberry frozen dessert or ice milk. Cover and freeze till firm. Store in freezer. Let stand at room temperature for 15 minutes before serving. To serve, garnish each serving with sliced banana and about 1 tablespoon Chocolate Dessert Sauce. Makes 8 servings.

CREAMY PINEAPPLE SHERBET

This creamy smooth sherbet has an intense pineapple flavor with honey undertones. The unusual addition of buttermilk gives it a certain richness and adds a pleasant tang, too.

25% fewer calories

80% less fat

¼	cup sugar	⅔	cup sugar
1	envelope unflavored gelatin	2	tablespoons honey
¼	cup cold water	1	teaspoon vanilla
1	15¼-ounce can crushed pineapple (juice pack)	2	cups low-fat buttermilk

Per Serving:

Calories	107
Total Fat	<1 g
Saturated fat	<1 g
Cholesterol	2 mg
Sodium	45 mg
Carbohydrate	25 g
Fiber	<1 g
Protein	2 g

In a small saucepan stir together ¼ cup sugar and gelatin; add water. Cook and stir over low heat till gelatin is dissolved. Remove from heat. Cool the mixture slightly.

❧

In a blender container or food processor bowl combine *undrained* pineapple, ⅔ cup sugar, honey, vanilla, and gelatin mixture. Cover and blend or process till smooth. (Process in batches if necessary.) Stir in buttermilk.

❧

Freeze the mixture in a 4-quart ice cream freezer according to the manufacturer's directions. Makes about 6 cups or 12 servings.

SHERBET RING WITH FRUIT

Instead of an ice cream ring drizzled with fudge sauce, make a three-layer rainbow sherbet ring and fill it with fruit. Enhance it further by serving one or more fruit sauces from pages 10 to 13.

Per Serving:

Calories	152
Total fat	2 g
Saturated fat	1 g
Cholesterol	7 mg
Sodium	47 mg
Carbohydrate	34 g
Fiber	1 g
Protein	1 g

1 pint raspberry sherbet, softened
1 pint lime sherbet, softened
1 pint orange sherbet, softened
1 cup honeydew melon balls
1 cup cantaloupe balls
1 cup strawberries, halved
½ cup blueberries or blackberries
Fresh mint leaves (optional)

Place a 6-cup ring mold in the freezer to chill for 10 minutes. Spoon raspberry sherbet into bottom of mold, spreading to smooth. Return to freezer till sherbet is firm. Repeat procedure with lime sherbet and orange sherbet. Cover and freeze till firm, at least 2 hours.

❧

To serve, dip mold into lukewarm water for about 5 seconds to loosen. Invert onto chilled serving plate and shake to release. Return to freezer to firm surface. Fill center with melon balls, strawberries, and blueberries or blackberries. Garnish with mint leaves, if desired. Makes 12 servings.

CHOCOLATE SUNDAES IN COOKIE CUPS

You can prepare the cookie cups a few days in advance. Just cool them and store in an airtight container. The cups are also delicious filled with a citrus sorbet or frozen nonfat yogurt.

45% fewer calories

75% less fat

No cholesterol

70% less sodium

Per Serving:

Calories	229
Total Fat	5 g
Saturated fat	1 g
Cholesterol	0 mg
Sodium	50 mg
Carbohydrate	41 g
Fiber	<1 g
Protein	4 g

Nonstick spray coating
¼ packed brown sugar
2 tablespoons light corn syrup
2 tablespoons margarine
¼ cup all-purpose flour
1 tablespoon finely chopped walnuts, toasted

1 quart vanilla ice milk or frozen nonfat yogurt
⅔ cup Chocolate Dessert Sauce (see recipe, page 10)
Sweet cherries (optional)

Spray a cookie sheet with nonstick coating; set pan aside.

In a small saucepan combine brown sugar, corn syrup, and margarine. Cook and stir over medium heat till mixture boils. Remove from heat. Stir in flour and walnuts; beat till smooth.

Spoon 1 level tablespoon batter for each cookie, about 6 inches apart onto prepared cookie sheet. (Place 2 cookies on each sheet.)

Bake in a 375° oven for 6 to 8 minutes or till cookies are set. Let cookies cool 1 to 2 minutes on baking sheet. (Cookies should be set but still flexible.) Remove carefully and drape cookies over inverted 6-ounce custard cups to cool. (If cookies are too firm to remove from baking sheets, place baking sheet back into oven for 15 to 20 seconds to soften.) Cool cookies completely. Let cookie sheet cool and spray with nonstick coating before baking 2 more cookies.

To serve, place scoops of ice milk or frozen yogurt in each cookie cup and top with Chocolate Dessert Sauce. Garnish with a cherry, if desired. Makes 8 servings.

STRAWBERRY BANANA FROZEN YOGURT

If you prefer, you can prepare the chilled mixture in a 2- or 3-quart ice cream freezer following the manufacturer's directions.

Per Serving:

Calories	98
Total Fat	<1 g
Saturated fat	0 g
Cholesterol	1 mg
Sodium	43 mg
Carbohydrate	20 g
Fiber	1 g
Protein	4 g

⅔ cup sugar
1 envelope unflavored gelatin
1 12-ounce can (1½ cups) evaporated skim milk
1 6-ounce carton banana low-fat yogurt
1 teaspoon vanilla
4 cups strawberries, hulled

In a small saucepan stir together the sugar and gelatin. Stir in evaporated skim milk. Cook and stir over low heat till gelatin is dissolved. Remove from heat. Stir in yogurt and vanilla.

❧

In a blender container or food processor bowl combine strawberries and gelatin mixture. Cover and blend till nearly smooth. (Process in batches if necessary.) Pour the mixture into a 9x9x2-inch baking pan. Cover and freeze about 4 hours or till almost firm.

❧

Break the frozen mixture into chunks. Transfer the chunks to a chilled, large mixing bowl. Beat with an electric mixer on medium speed till smooth but not melted. Return quickly to the chilled pan. Cover and freeze about 3 hours or till firm.

❧

To serve, let frozen yogurt stand at room temperature for 10 to 15 minutes to soften. Makes about 6 cups or 12 servings.

RAINBOW ANGEL CAKE

You'll need a 10-inch cake for this light and airy dessert. Prepare the cake from scratch or use a mix.

1 16-ounce package frozen unsweetened strawberries, thawed
3 tablespoons sugar
1 teaspoon finely shredded lemon peel
3 tablespoons lemon juice
1 10-inch angel food cake

1 pint frozen lime sherbet, softened
1 pint frozen raspberry sherbet, softened
1 pint frozen lemon sherbet, softened
1 1.3-ounce envelope whipped dessert topping mix
½ cup skim milk
½ teaspoon vanilla

Per Serving:

Calories	244
Total fat	2 g
Saturated fat	1 g
Cholesterol	7 mg
Sodium	119 mg
Carbohydrate	53 g
Fiber	1 g
Protein	3 g

For sauce, in a 2-quart saucepan combine *undrained* strawberries, sugar, lemon peel, and lemon juice. Cook and stir till mixture comes to a boil and sugar dissolves. Remove from heat. Press mixture through a sieve to remove seeds. Cool thoroughly.

Split cake horizontally into four equal layers. To assemble, place the bottom cake layer on serving plate. Spread with lime sherbet to within ½ inch of edge. Top with second cake layer; cover and freeze for 45 minutes.

Spread second cake layer with raspberry sherbet. Add third cake layer; cover and freeze for 45 minutes. Spread third cake layer with lemon sherbet; top with remaining cake layer. Cover and freeze till firm.

Meanwhile, prepare whipped dessert topping with skim milk and vanilla according to package directions. Spread prepared topping on top of cake. Cover and freeze for 4 hours or up to 3 days.

To serve, let stand at room temperature for 10 minutes to soften before cutting. Serve with strawberry sauce. Refrigerate any leftover strawberry sauce and keep leftover cake in the freezer. Makes 12 servings.

CHOCOLATE ICE CREAM CAKE

An impressive dessert for a special occasion. Its a snap to prepare, too, because it starts with a cake mix and can be made in advance.

Per Serving:

Calories	*346*
Total fat	*7 g*
Saturated fat	*4 g*
Cholesterol	*36 mg*
Sodium	*329 mg*
Carbohydrate	*63 g*
Fiber	*1 g*
Protein	*7 g*

Nonstick spray coating
1 package 2-layer-size regular chocolate cake mix
1⅓ cups water
½ cup plain nonfat yogurt
4 egg whites
1 quart cherry-nut ice milk, softened

1 pint chocolate ice milk, softened
1 1.3-ounce envelope whipped dessert topping mix
1 tablespoon unsweetened cocoa powder
½ cup skim milk
1 teaspoon vanilla

Spray two 8x1½-inch round baking pans with nonstick coating. Set aside.

Prepare cake mix, using 1⅓ cups water, yogurt, and egg whites instead of ingredients called for on the package, but otherwise follow package directions. Divide batter equally between prepared pans. Bake in a 350° oven for 35 to 40 minutes or till a toothpick inserted near the center comes out clean. Cool in pans on wire racks for 10 minutes. Remove from pans; cool completely on racks.

Slice each cake in half horizontally making four layers. To assemble cake, place one layer on serving plate; spread with *half* of cherry-nut ice milk; top with second layer. Spread with chocolate ice milk; top with third layer. Spread with remaining cherry-nut ice milk; top with last layer. Cover and freeze for 1 hour.

In a medium bowl combine dessert topping mix, cocoa powder, milk, and vanilla. Beat with an electric mixer on high speed till thickened and of spreading consistency. Spread sides and top of cake with whipped topping mixture. Cover and freeze till firm.

To serve, remove cake from freezer about 10 minutes before serving. If desired, sprinkle top lightly with cocoa powder. Cut into wedges using a wet knife. Makes 12 servings.

APRICOT ICE MILK SQUARES

A versatile dessert idea that's also good made with chocolate wafers and other lower sugar spreads such as strawberry or raspberry.

1 cup crushed vanilla wafers
   (22 wafers)
2 tablespoons margarine, melted
½ teaspoon almond extract

¼ cup chopped almonds, toasted
1 quart vanilla ice milk
1 cup lower sugar apricot spread

Per Serving:

Calories	212
Total fat	8 g
Saturated fat	2 g
Cholesterol	14 mg
Sodium	101 mg
Carbohydrate	32 g
Fiber	1 g
Protein	4 g

In a small mixing bowl combine crushed vanilla wafers, margarine, and almond extract; mix well. Reserve ¼ *cup* crumb mixture. Press remaining crumb mixture in bottom of 2-quart square baking dish. Bake in a 375° oven for 5 minutes. Cool completely on a wire rack. Stir almonds into reserved crumb mixture; set aside.

Scoop ice milk into a chilled bowl. Stir and press ice milk against side of bowl with the back of a spoon to soften. When softened, add apricot spread; stir just to marble. Spread over the cooled crust. Top with reserved crumb-almond mixture. Cover with foil. Freeze several hours or till firm. To serve, cut into squares. Makes 9 servings.

LIME VANILLA CRUNCH PIE

A wedge of this frozen pie is a welcome dessert on hot, humid days. The flavor is light and adds a lift to the meal.

Per Serving:

Calories	191
Total fat	4 g
Saturated fat	2 g
Cholesterol	6 mg
Sodium	115 mg
Carbohydrate	37 g
Fiber	<1 g
Protein:	3 g

1   cup cornflake crumbs
¼   cup flaked coconut
2   tablespoons honey
2   tablespoon margarine, melted

1   quart lime or orange sherbet, softened
1   pint vanilla fat-free frozen dessert, softened

In a bowl combine cornflake crumbs, coconut, honey, and margarine. Mix well. Press mixture into bottom and sides of 9-inch pie plate. Freeze for 10 minutes to set crumb shell.

≈

Using the back of a spoon or spatula, carefully spread sherbet as evenly as possible on the crumb shell and up the sides to form another shell. Place in freezer for 15 minutes or till firm.

≈

Spoon frozen dessert into center to fill the pie. Cover and freeze about 2 hours or till firm.

≈

To serve, cut into wedges. Serve with your favorite fruit sauce, if desired. Makes 10 servings.

GINGERED PEAR SORBET DESSERT

No ice cream freezer is needed for this lightly spiced pear sorbet—it freezes to perfection right in your home freezer.

90% less fat

no cholesterol

⅔ cup water
⅔ cup sugar
4 medium pears, peeled, cored and sliced (4 cups)
2 tablespoons chopped crystallized ginger

2 tablespoons brandy or apple juice
¼ teaspoon ground cinnamon
1 small cantaloupe, cut crosswise into 6 rings and seeded
Fresh berries

Per Serving:

Calories	234
Total Fat	1 g
Saturated fat	0 g
Cholesterol	0 mg
Sodium	29 mg
Carbohydrate	57 g
Fiber	6 g
Protein	2 g

In a small saucepan combine the water and sugar. Bring to boiling. Remove from heat. Cool thoroughly. Cover and chill.

❧

Place the pears and ginger in a blender container or food processor bowl. Add the chilled syrup mixture, brandy or apple juice, and cinnamon. Cover and blend or process till smooth. Transfer mixture to an 8x4x2- or a 9x5x3-inch loaf pan. Cover and freeze about 3 hours or till almost firm.

❧

Break the frozen mixture into small chunks. Transfer chunks to a chilled mixing bowl. Beat with an electric mixer on medium speed till smooth but not melted. Return quickly to the chilled pan. Cover and freeze overnight or till firm.

❧

To serve, let stand at room temperature for 15 to 20 minutes. Place cantaloupe rings on dessert plates, top with a scoop of sorbet and fresh berries. Makes about 3 cups or 6 servings.

CHERRY-ALMOND TORTONI CUPS

This recipe can also double as a frozen salad served on a lettuce leaf. Any favorite cookie, from gingersnap to oatmeal, will make a fine topping for these tortoni cups.

70% fewer calories

85% less fat

95% less cholesterol

1 8-ounce carton vanilla nonfat yogurt
¼ teaspoon almond extract
1 cup reduced-fat frozen whipped dessert topping, thawed
1 8-ounce can crushed pineapple, drained

1 banana, diced
2 tablespoons finely chopped pecans, toasted
1 16-ounce can pitted sweet cherries, drained and chopped
¼ cup crumbled macaroons

Per Serving:

Calories	73
Total fat	3 g
Saturated fat	<1 g
Cholesterol	1 mg
Sodium	17 mg
Carbohydrate	13 g
Fiber	<1 g
Protein	1 g

Line twelve 2½-inch muffin cups with paper bake cups; set aside.

In a medium bowl combine yogurt and almond extract. Fold in whipped topping. Then fold in drained pineapple, banana, and pecans. Blot cherries with paper towels. Gently fold into yogurt mixture. Spoon about ⅓ *cup* mixture into each prepared muffin cup. Sprinkle with crumbled macaroons. Cover and freeze about 2 to 3 hours or till firm. Let stand 10 to 15 minutes before serving. Makes 12 servings.

FROZEN ZUCCOTTO

The original recipe for Italian Zuccotto that inspired this recipe is filled with a mix of whipped cream, chopped chocolate, and nuts. We hope you'll like our lightened version because you can store it in your freezer.

Per Serving:

Calories	174
Total fat	3 g
Saturated fat	1 g
Cholesterol	46 mg
Sodium	55 mg
Carbohydrate	32 g
Fiber	<1 g
Protein	3 g

Simply Delicious Citrus Sponge Cake (see recipe, page 90)
⅔ cup orange juice
⅓ cup sugar
1 pint orange sherbet, softened
1 pint chocolate ice milk or frozen nonfat yogurt, softened
1 pint strawberry ice milk or frozen nonfat yogurt, softened
Whipped Topping or Whipped Milk Topping (see recipes, page 9) or Raspberry Sauce (see recipe, page 12)

Prepare Simply Delicious Citrus Sponge Cake as directed. (Do not prepare filling.)

❧

Line a 2½-quart bowl with plastic wrap. Cut cake into ¼-inch-wide strips. Stir together orange juice and sugar till sugar is dissolved. Brush both sides of one cake strip with the syrup mixture. Place strip against bottom and sides of the prepared bowl. Continue brushing and arranging strips in bowl till bowl is completely lined, cutting strips to fit. Freeze for 30 minutes.

❧

Spread sherbet in cake-lined bowl. Spread chocolate ice milk or yogurt over sherbet layer. Then spread strawberry ice milk or yogurt over chocolate layer. Brush remaining cake strips with remaining syrup mixture and place atop strawberry layer, cutting as necessary to cover. Trim edges. Cover and freeze for 6 hours or till firm.

❧

To serve, unmold onto platter. Garnish with Whipped Topping, Whipped Milk Topping, or Raspberry Sauce. Cut into wedges to serve. (If necessary, let stand 5 minutes before slicing.) Makes 16 servings.

STRAWBERRY BOMBES WITH CINNAMON-BLUEBERRY SAUCE

A light, easy, and refreshing party dessert that's easy on the cook. You can vary the flavor of frozen yogurt and choose any one of the other fruit sauces in this book.

1   cup fresh or frozen blueberries, thawed
1   quart strawberry frozen nonfat yogurt, softened

Cinnamon Blueberry Sauce
(see recipe, page 12)

Chill 8 fluted 4-ounce molds or custard cups. Stir blueberries into softened strawberry yogurt. Spoon yogurt mixture into each mold. Cover and freeze about 2 hours or till firm.

To serve, dip molds into lukewarm water for about 2 seconds to loosen. Invert onto chilled baking sheet and return to freezer to firm surface. On each chilled dessert dish, place a strawberry bombe and serve with Cinnamon Blueberry Sauce. Makes 8 servings.

FRUIT DESSERTS

If you favor the simplicity of fresh fruit for dessert, try Summer Fruits with Ricotta Dip or layer upon layer of fruit in the Heavenly Ambrosia. Whipped toppings embellish both the Fiesta Pineapple and Mocha Nectarines without adding a lot of calories. Or try a pear recipe–glazed with orange marmalade, bathed in chocolate sauce, or arranged in a peach sauce flavored with white wine. This chapter's recipes average only about 130 calories and have 1 gram or less of saturated fat per serving.

CHOCOLATE SAUCED PEARS

When you feel like a chocolate binge, but can't afford the extra calories—make up these baked pears. They're less than 150 calories per serving and have only 1 gram of fat.

25% fewer calories

4 small pears
2 tablespoons lemon juice
2 teaspoons vanilla

½ teaspoon ground cinnamon
2 tablespoons chocolate-flavored
  syrup

Core pears from bottom end, leaving stems intact. Peel pears. If necessary, cut a thin slice from bottoms of pears to help stand upright.

❧

Place pears in a 2-quart square baking dish. Stir together lemon juice, vanilla, and cinnamon. Brush onto pears. Pour any extra lemon juice mixture over pears.

❧

Bake, covered, in a 375° oven for 30 to 35 minutes or till pears are tender. Cool slightly.

❧

To serve, place warm pears, stem end up, on dessert plates. Strain baking liquid; pour liquid into a small bowl. Stir in chocolate-flavored syrup. Drizzle over pears. Serve warm. Makes 4 servings.

Per Serving:

Calories	*134*
Total fat	*1 g*
Saturated fat	*<1 g*
Cholesterol	*0 g*
Sodium	*6 mg*
Carbohydrate	*34 g*
Fiber	*5 g*
Protein	*1 g*

MARMALADE-GLAZED PEARS

Something as simple as poached pears makes an impressive display when glazed with orange marmalade, served in a pretty crystal dish, and garnished with a mint leaf. (For the nutritional analysis we compared this recipe to pears served in a butter and cream sauce.)

Per Serving:

Calories	*129*
Total fat	*1 g*
Saturated fat	*<1 g*
Cholesterol	*0 mg*
Sodium	*4 mg*
Carbohydrate	*33 g*
Fiber	*4 g*
Protein	*1 g*

2   teaspoons finely shredded
    orange peel
½   cup orange juice
¼   cup water

4   medium pears
⅓   cup low-sugar orange
    marmalade spread
Fresh mint leaves (optional)

In a 2-quart saucepan combine orange peel, orange juice, and water; bring to boiling.

Meanwhile, core pears from bottom end, leaving stems intact. Peel pears. Add pears, stem end up, to saucepan. Simmer, covered, 10 to 20 minutes or till just tender. Using a slotted spoon remove pears to individual dessert dishes, placing them stem end up. Discard liquid from saucepan; add marmalade to pan. Heat just till marmalade melts; spoon over pears to glaze. Cover and chill thoroughly. Garnish each pear with a mint leaf, if desired. Makes 4 servings.

FIESTA PINEAPPLE

Choose the ripest pineapple you can find because it won't ripen after picking. You should be able to pull a leaf easily from the center of the crown. For the photo, we turned the crown so the leafy side was up.

Per Serving:

Calories	179
Total fat	5 g
Saturated fat	<1 g
Cholesterol	<1 mg
Sodium	16 mg
Carbohydrate	36 g
Fiber	2 g
Protein	1 g

1 whole pineapple
1 tablespoon light or dark rum or orange juice plus several drops rum flavoring
1 cup reduced-fat frozen whipped dessert topping, thawed

1 kiwi fruit, peeled and cut into 12 half-slices
¼ cup peach preserves
1 tablespoon light or dark rum or orange juice plus several drops rum flavoring

Cut pineapple into quarters lengthwise through the crown, using a sharp knife. Remove core from each quarter. Then cut between shell and fruit, separating fruit from the shell in one piece. Leaving fruit in place, cut into 6 to 8 crosswise pieces. Push slices in alternate directions to give a zigzag pattern. Repeat with remaining pineapple quarters.

✿

Brush surface of pineapple slices with 1 tablespoon rum or orange-rum mixture. Top each serving with whipped topping and 3 kiwi fruit half-slices. In a small bowl combine peach preserves and 1 tablespoon rum or orange-rum mixture to make of drizzling consistency. Drizzle on each pineapple quarter. Makes 4 servings.

MOCHA NECTARINES

It's easy to make loose chocolate curls as in the photo. Just pull a vegetable peeler along one edge of the chocolate with quick, short flicks of the wrist. For nutritional analysis we compared the recipe to a sour cream and nut-topped nectarine dessert.

4 medium nectarines	½ ounce semisweet chocolate, cut into curls
1 tablespoon coffee liqueur	
1 cup reduced-fat frozen whipped dessert topping, thawed	2 tablespoons chopped pecans, toasted

Holding nectarines stem end down, cut each into 8 equal wedges, cutting to about ½ inch from the stem end. Gently pull out pit and discard.

❧

Place opened nectarines on dessert plates. In small bowl gradually stir coffee liqueur into whipped topping. Spoon coffee mixture into each nectarine. Garnish each with chocolate curls and toasted pecans. Makes 4 servings.

BAKED APPLE WEDGES

Similar to a baked apple in flavor, this version is light and is compared with an apple crisp. It's delightful served with frozen yogurt or a pour of skim milk.

Per Serving:

Calories	196
Total Fat	5 g
Saturated fat	1 g
Cholesterol	0 mg
Sodium	51 mg
Carbohydrate	40 g
Fiber	1 g
Protein	1 g

Nonstick spray coating
6 medium cooking apples, peeled, each cut into 6 wedges, and cored
1 tablespoon granulated sugar
½ teaspoon ground cinnamon
½ cup packed brown sugar
⅓ cup all-purpose flour
⅛ teaspoon ground nutmeg
2 tablespoons margarine, melted

Spray a 2-quart rectangular baking dish with nonstick coating. In a large bowl toss apples with granulated sugar and cinnamon. Place in prepared baking dish. Bake, covered, in a 350° oven for 30 minutes.

Meanwhile, in a small bowl combine the brown sugar, flour, and nutmeg. Add the margarine, stirring with a fork till mixture is crumbly. Uncover dish and sprinkle brown sugar mixture over apples.

Bake for 15 to 20 minutes more or till apples are tender. Serve warm. Makes 6 servings.

CRANBERRY PEAR COMPOTE

The next morning you can enjoy any leftovers of this recipe for breakfast.

45% fewer calories

---

8 whole cloves
3 inches stick cinnamon
¾ cup water
½ cup sugar
1 teaspoon finely shredded
   lemon peel

1¾ pounds pears, peeled, cored,
    and sliced ¼-inch thick (6
    cups)
2   cups cranberries

Per Serving:

Calories	149
Total Fat	1 g
Saturated fat	<1 g
Cholesterol	0 mg
Sodium	2 mg
Carbohydrate	38 g
Fiber	3 g
Protein	1 g

For spice bag, cut a double thickness of 100% cotton cheesecloth into a 6- to 8-inch square. Place cloves and cinnamon stick in the center of the cheesecloth. Bring up corners of cheesecloth and tie with a clean string.

🍂

In a 3-quart saucepan heat water, sugar, spice bag, and lemon peel. Bring to boiling. Add pears and cranberries; return to boiling. Reduce heat. Simmer, covered, 10 minutes or till fruit is softened. Remove from heat; transfer to serving dish. Cover and chill at least 2 hours.

🍂

Before serving, remove spice bag and spoon fruit into dessert dishes. Makes 6 servings.

MAPLE APPLES

Sweet and delicious, baked apples satisfy your family's sweet tooth and supply some nutritional benefits, too.

Per Serving:

Calories _____ 150
Total Fat _____ 3 g
  Saturated fat _____ < 1 g
Cholesterol _____ 0 mg
Sodium _____ 25mg
Carbohydrate _____ 34g
Fiber _____ 4g
Protein _____ 1 g

4 medium cooking apples, cored
¼ cup raisins or dried cranberries
2 tablespoons chopped walnuts

3 tablespoons reduced-calorie maple-flavored syrup
½ cup water

Cut off a strip of peel near the top of each apple. Arrange apples in a 2-quart square baking dish. Fill apples with raisins or cranberries and walnuts. Brush apples with syrup. Add the water to the baking dish.

❧

Bake in a 350° oven for 40 to 45 minutes or till apples are tender, basting occasionally with the cooking liquid. Serve warm. Makes 4 servings.

PEACHY POACHED PEARS

The pretty color of this simple peach sauce spiked with white wine makes this dessert special enough for company.

20% fewer calories

Per Serving:

Calories _____ 132
Total Fat _____ 1 g
 Saturated fat _____ <1 g
Cholesterol _____ 0 mg
Sodium _____ 5 mg
Carbohydrate _____ 31 g
Fiber _____ 4 g
Protein _____ 1 g

1 16-ounce can peach slices in
    extra light syrup
   White wine
3 inches stick cinnamon
¼ teaspoon ground ginger

3 large pears, peeled, halved,
    and cored
2 tablespoons honey
   Fresh mint sprigs (optional)
   Fresh berries (optional)

Drain peaches; reserve syrup. Set peaches aside. Add enough wine to syrup to make 1 cup. In a large skillet combine syrup mixture, cinnamon, and ginger; bring to boiling. Add pears. Reduce heat. Simmer, covered, for 10 to 15 minutes or till pears are tender. Using a slotted spoon remove pears. Discard cinnamon. Reserve poaching liquid.

❧

For sauce, place peaches and honey in a blender container or food processor bowl. Cover and blend or process till pureed. Stir in enough of the reserved poaching liquid to make 1½ cups sauce. Cover and chill pears and sauce separately in the refrigerator till serving time.

❧

To serve, spoon the peach sauce onto 6 serving plates. Cut each pear half lengthwise into thin slices, cutting almost, but not quite through the top of the pear. Arrange each pear half on peach sauce, fanning the slices. If desired, garnish with a sprig of mint and fresh berries. Makes 6 servings.

HONEY AND SPICE FRUIT COMPOTE

Because fruits are naturally sweet, they usually require little additional sugar or other sweeteners to serve for dessert. Here we've poached dried and fresh fruits together and used light sour cream in the topping to cut fat and calories.

20% fewer calories

85% less fat

Sour Cream Topping
½ of an 8-ounce package mixed dried fruit
3 small apples or pears, peeled, cored, and sliced
2 cups water
½ cup raisins
3 tablespoons apple juice or orange juice
1 tablespoon honey
1 teaspoon cornstarch
½ teaspoon apple pie spice
Ground nutmeg (optional)
6 lemon peel curls (optional)

Per Serving:

Calories	*163*
Total fat	*1 g*
Saturated fat	*1 g*
Cholesterol	*2 mg*
Sodium	*25 mg*
Carbohydrate	*40 g*
Fiber	*1 g*
Protein	*2 g*

Prepare Sour Cream Topping; cover and chill.

❧

Cut up large pieces of dried fruit. In a medium saucepan combine dried fruit, apples or pears, water and raisins. Bring to boiling; reduce heat. Simmer, covered, 6 to 8 minutes or till fruit is just tender, stirring once or twice.

❧

Stir together the apple or orange juice, honey, cornstarch, and apple pie spice. Stir into fruit mixture. Cook and stir till thickened and bubbly. Cook and stir for 1 minute more. Serve warm or cover and chill till serving time.

To serve, top each serving with Sour Cream Topping. Sprinkle with nutmeg and garnish with lemon peel curl, if desired. Makes 6 servings.

SOUR CREAM TOPPING: In a small bowl combine ⅓ cup *light dairy sour cream*, 2 tablespoons *brown sugar*, and ½ teaspoon *vanilla*. Cover and chill till serving time.

ORANGES IN CARAMEL SYRUP

Here's an easy make-ahead dessert you can prepare year-round. It's the perfect ending for a holiday meal when a light refreshing dessert is a must.

55% fewer calories

Per Serving:

Calories	132
Total fat	<1 g
Saturated fat	<1 g
Cholesterol	0 mg
Sodium	1 mg
Carbohydrate	31 g
Fiber	3 g
Protein	1 g

EXTRA-LIGHT

½   cup sugar
1   cup warm water
2   tablespoons light rum or
    ¼ teaspoon rum flavoring

6   medium navel oranges
    Fresh red raspberries
    (optional)
    Fresh mint leaves (optional)

Place sugar in a heavy small skillet. Heat over medium-high heat till sugar begins to melt, shaking skillet occasionally to heat sugar evenly. Do not stir. Reduce heat to low; cook till sugar is melted and golden (about 5 minutes more). Stir as necessary after sugar begins to melt and as mixture bubbles. Remove from heat. Slowly pour in the warm water. Return to heat and cook on low heat till caramel dissolves. Slowly stir in rum or rum flavoring. Bring to boiling; reduce heat. Simmer for 5 minutes. Cool.

❧

Using a vegetable peeler, remove the peel from one orange. Cut peel into julienne strips and add to caramel syrup. Using a sharp paring knife, remove the peel and white membrane from all the oranges.

❧

Slice oranges and place in a shallow dish. Pour caramel syrup over oranges. Cover and chill at least 2 hours or overnight. To serve, place orange slices in dessert dishes. Spoon caramel syrup over oranges and garnish with fresh raspberries and mint leaves, if desired. Makes 6 servings.

70% fewer calories

95% less fat

90% less cholesterol

80% less sodium

SUMMER FRUITS WITH RICOTTA DIP

This recipe was doubled for the photo and makes a terrific summertime dessert for outdoor buffets or barbecues.

Per Serving:

Calories_____101
Total fat_____1 g
  Saturated fat_____<1 g
Cholesterol_____3 mg
Sodium_____26 mg
Carbohydrate_____21 g
Fiber_____1 g
Protein_____4 g

⅓ cup nonfat ricotta cheese
2 tablespoons sugar
1 teaspoon finely shredded
    lemon or orange peel
1 tablespoon orange juice

⅓ cup vanilla low-fat yogurt
2 cups sliced plums, cubed
    cantaloupe, cubed
    honeydew melon, dark
    sweet cherries, and/or
    strawberries

For dip, in a blender container or food processor bowl combine ricotta cheese, sugar, lemon or orange peel, and orange juice. Cover and blend or process till smooth. Stir cheese mixture into the yogurt. If desired, cover and chill dip up to 24 hours.

❧

Serve with assorted fresh fruit. Garnish dip with additional finely shredded orange peel, if desired. Makes 4 servings.

HEAVENLY AMBROSIA

Traditional ambrosia is made with oranges, bananas, and coconut. Layer your favorite fruit combination into the serving dish and top with the strawberry puree.

55% fewer calories

½ cup medium strawberries, hulled
1 tablespoon honey
½ teaspoon finely shredded orange peel
1 pink grapefruit

2 medium oranges
1 cup halved seedless green grapes
1 cup medium strawberries, hulled
2 tablespoons coconut, toasted

Per Serving:

Calories	*70*
Total Fat	*1 g*
Saturated fat	*<1 g*
Cholesterol	*0 mg*
Sodium	*4 mg*
Carbohydrate	*16 g*
Fiber	*2 g*
Protein	*1 g*

In blender container or food processor bowl combine ½ cup strawberries, honey, and orange peel. Set aside.

Over a bowl, peel and section grapefruit, reserving juice. Peel oranges and cut into half-slices, reserving juice. Set fruit aside.

Add reserved juices to strawberry mixture. Cover and blend or process till smooth. In 2-quart glass serving bowl layer grapefruit sections, halved grapes, orange slices, and 1 cup strawberries. Pour pureed strawberry mixture over all. Cover and chill till serving time. Top with toasted coconut. Makes 6 servings.

MARGARITA FRUIT COMPOTE

A ripe pineapple can range in color from yellow to a rich gold. If you need to store it for a day or two, place it in a plastic bag and refrigerate.

Per Serving:

Calories _____ 130
Total fat _____ 1 g
  Saturated fat _____ <1 g
Cholesterol _____ 0 mg
Sodium _____ 2 mg
Carbohydrate _____ 33 g
Fiber _____ 3 g
Protein _____ 1 g

EXTRA-LIGHT

1	medium pineapple	1	cup seedless red grapes
2	medium nectarines, pitted and sliced	¼	cup frozen margarita mix, thawed
2	small apples, cored and sliced	¼	cup water
2	plums, pitted and sliced	1	medium banana, sliced

To make two pineapple boats, cut pineapple in half lengthwise through the crown, using a sharp knife. Remove fruit with curved knife, leaving shells intact. Remove core from fruit; cut fruit into chunks. Cover and reserve pineapple boats.

❧

In a large bowl combine pineapple chunks, nectarine slices, apple slices, plum slices, and grapes. In a small bowl combine margarita mix and water. Pour over fruit mixture; toss gently to mix. Cover; chill till serving time.

❧

Just before serving, slice banana into fruit mixture; toss gently. To serve, use pineapple boats as serving bowls. Makes 6 servings.

Fresh Fruit Layered Parfaits

Light, refreshing, and colorful, this dessert choice is always welcome, particularly during the hot, humid summer months.

50% fewer calories

1 envelope unflavored gelatin
2 cups apple juice
1 tablespoon snipped fresh mint
1 teaspoon vanilla
⅔ cup chopped seeded watermelon or honeydew melon

⅔ cup chopped, peeled peaches or chopped nectarines or chopped cantaloupe
⅔ cup sliced strawberries
⅔ cup blueberries
Whipped Topping or Whipped Milk Topping (see recipes, page 9) (optional)
Fresh mint sprigs (optional)

Per Serving:

Calories	55
Total fat	<1 g
Saturated fat	<1 g
Cholesterol	0 mg
Sodium	4 mg
Carbohydrate	13 g
Fiber	1 g
Protein	1 g

In a small saucepan sprinkle gelatin over *½ cup* of the apple juice. Let stand 5 minutes. Cook and stir over low heat till gelatin dissolves. Stir in the remaining apple juice, mint, and vanilla. Chill till partially set (the consistency of unbeaten egg whites).

❧

In each of 8 parfait glasses layer the watermelon or honeydew melon, peaches, strawberries, and blueberries. Spoon gelatin mixture over all. Cover and chill for 4 to 24 hours or till set.

❧

If desired, garnish each parfait with Whipped Topping and a fresh mint sprig. Makes 8 servings.

FRUIT WITH YOGURT TOPPING

The little orange peel garnish adds a nice touch to this simple dessert. Use a zester to remove a 2-inch-long strip of orange peel and tie into a bow. The recipe was compared to a fruit mixture topped with a coconut cream mixture.

25% fewer calories

90% less fat

Per Serving:

Calories_____127
Total fat_____1 g
 Saturated fat_____<1 g
Cholesterol_____4 mg
Sodium_____119 mg
Carbohydrate_____27 g
Fiber_____3 g
Protein_____5 g

½ cup vanilla low-fat yogurt
¼ cup fat-free cream cheese
    product
½ teaspoon finely shredded
    orange peel
2 oranges, peeled and sectioned

2 cups strawberries, hulled and
    halved
1 cup fresh pineapple chunks
1 cup seedless green grapes
    Lemon leaves (optional)

For topping, in a small bowl combine yogurt, cream cheese product, and orange peel. Beat with a spoon till smooth. Cover and chill till serving time.

❧

In a large bowl combine orange sections, strawberries, pineapple chunks, and green grapes. Spoon mixture into dessert dishes. Serve with yogurt topping. Garnish with lemon leaves, if desired. Makes 4 servings.

SPICED FRESH FRUIT BOWL

Simple pleasures are often the best. This fresh fruit combo is coated with a lightly spiced sugar syrup.

Per Serving:

Calories	97
Total Fat	<1 g
Saturated fat	<1 g
Cholesterol	0 mg
Sodium	2 mg
Carbohydrate	24 g
Fiber	3 g
Protein	1 g

½ cup water
¼ cup sugar
2 teaspoons lemon juice
3 whole cloves
2 inches stick cinnamon

4 cups mixed fresh fruit (orange slices, pineapple chunks, halved strawberries, seedless green grapes, chopped apple, sliced peaches, and/or sliced plums)

In a small saucepan combine water, sugar, lemon juice, cloves, and cinnamon. Bring to boiling; reduce heat. Simmer, covered, for 10 minutes. Cool to room temperature. Remove and discard spices.

❧

Combine fresh fruit in a 2-quart glass serving bowl. Add cooled syrup, stirring carefully to coat. Cover and chill in the refrigerator for 4 hours or till very cold, stirring occasionally. Makes 6 servings.

SAUTÉED CINNAMON BANANAS

Check the label on the frozen yogurt carefully. Not all frozen yogurt is low-calorie or even low in fat. We used frozen nonfat yogurt when we did the nutrition analysis for this recipe. This recipe is a slimmed-down version of Bananas Foster.

65% fewer calories

80% less fat

no cholesterol

60% less sodium

3	bananas
2	tablespoons margarine
¼	cup packed brown sugar

2	tablespoons water
¼	teaspoon ground cinnamon
2	cups vanilla frozen nonfat yogurt

Per Serving:

Calories	*174*
Total Fat	*4 g*
Saturated fat	*1 g*
Cholesterol	*0 mg*
Sodium	*88 mg*
Carbohydrate	*35 g*
Fiber	*1 g*
Protein	*3 g*

Peel bananas; halve crosswise, then lengthwise. In a large skillet melt margarine over medium heat. Add bananas. Cook about 2 minutes, stirring gently, till bananas are warm and softened. Add brown sugar, water, and cinnamon. Cook and stir till sugar melts; be careful not to break up bananas.

⮞

Serve warm over frozen yogurt. Makes 6 servings.

PEACH-RASPBERRY YOGURT CREAM

A low-fat dessert alternative layered with naturally sweet peaches, delicate raspberries, and honeyed vanilla yogurt. It's gently heated and sprinkled with brown sugar before serving.

85% less fat

Per Serving:

Calories	*136*
Total Fat	*<1 g*
Saturated fat	*<1 g*
Cholesterol	*1 mg*
Sodium	*37 mg*
Carbohydrate	*32 g*
Fiber	*3 g*
Protein	*4 g*

EXTRA-LIGHT

2   medium peaches, peeled, pitted, and sliced
1   teaspoon lemon juice
2   cups fresh raspberries

1   tablespoon raspberry or almond liqueur (optional)
1   cup vanilla nonfat yogurt
1   tablespoon honey
2   tablespoons brown sugar

In a medium bowl toss peaches with lemon juice. Gently toss in raspberries and liqueur, if desired. Spoon mixture into four 8-ounce ramekins. In a small bowl combine yogurt and honey. Spoon over fruit mixture. Cover and chill in the refrigerator till serving time, at least 1 hour.

❧

To serve, bake in a 500° oven for 7 to 10 minutes or till fruit is warm. Sprinkle with brown sugar. Serve immediately. Makes 4 servings.

INDEX

METRIC EQUIVALENTS

METRIC COOKING HINTS

By making a few conversions, cooks in Australia, Canada, and the United Kingdom can use the recipes in Better Homes and Gardens® *Favorite Desserts Made Lighter* with confidence. The charts on this page provide a guide for converting measurements from the U.S. customary system, which is used throughout this book, to the imperial and metric systems. There also is a conversion table for oven temperatures to accommodate the differences in oven calibrations.

Volume and Weight: Americans traditionally use cup measures for liquid and solid ingredients. The chart (top right) shows the approximate imperial and metric equivalents. If you are accustomed to weighing solid ingredients, here are some helpful approximate equivalents.

■ 1 cup butter, caster sugar, or rice = 8 ounces = about 250 grams
■ 1 cup flour = 4 ounces = about 125 grams
■ 1 cup icing sugar = 5 ounces = about 150 grams

Spoon measures are used for smaller amounts of ingredients. Although the size of the tablespoon varies slightly among countries. However, for practical purposes and for recipes in this book, a straight substitution is all that's necessary.

Measurements made using cups or spoons should always be level, unless stated otherwise.

Product Differences: Most of the ingredients called for in the recipes in this book are available in English-speaking countries. However, some are known by different names. Here are some common American ingredients and their possible counterparts:

■ Sugar is granulated or caster sugar.
■ Powdered sugar is icing sugar.
■ All-purpose flour is plain household flour or white flour. When self-rising flour is used in place of all-purpose flour in a recipe that calls for leavening, omit the leavening agent (baking soda or baking powder) and salt.
■ Light corn syrup is golden syrup.
■ Cornstarch is cornflour.
■ Baking soda is bicarbonate of soda.
■ Vanilla is vanilla essence.

USEFUL EQUIVALENTS

⅛ teaspoon = 0.5 ml
¼ teaspoon = 1 ml
½ teaspoon = 2 ml
1 teaspoon = 5 ml
¼ cup = 2 fluid ounces = 50 ml
⅓ cup = 3 fluid ounces = 75 ml
½ cup = 4 fluid ounces = 125 ml

⅔ cup = 5 fluid ounces = 150 ml
¾ cup = 6 fluid ounces = 175 ml
1 cup = 8 fluid ounces = 250 ml
2 cups = 1 pint
2 pints = 1 litre
½ inch = 1 centimetre
1 inch = 2 centimetres

BAKING PAN SIZES

American	Metric
8x1½-inch round baking pan	20x4-centimetre sandwich or cake tin
9x1½-inch round baking pan	23x3.5-centimetre sandwich or cake tin
11x7x1½-inch baking pan	28x18x4-centimetre baking pan
13x9x2-inch baking pan	32.5x23x5-centimetre baking pan
2-quart rectangular baking dish	30x19x5-centimetre baking pan
15x10x2-inch baking pan	38x25.5x2.5-centimetre baking pan (Swiss roll tin)
9-inch pie plate	22x4- or 23x4-centimetre pie plate
7- or 8-inch springform pan	18- or 20-centimetre springform or loose-bottom cake tin
9x5x3-inch loaf pan	23x13x6-centimetre or 2-pound narrow loaf pan or paté tin
1½-quart casserole	1.5-litre casserole
2-quart casserole	2-litre casserole

OVEN TEMPERATURE EQUIVALENTS

Fahrenheit Setting	Celsius Setting*	Gas Setting
300°F	150°C	Gas Mark 2
325°F	160°C	Gas Mark 3
350°F	180°C	Gas Mark 4
375°F	190°C	Gas Mark 5
400°F	200°C	Gas Mark 6
425°F	220°C	Gas Mark 7
450°F	230°C	Gas Mark 8
Broil		Grill

Electric and gas ovens may be calibrated using Celsius. However, increase the Celsius setting 10 to 20 degrees when cooking above 160°C with an electric oven. For convection or forced-air ovens (gas or electric), lower the temperature setting 10°C when cooking at all heat levels.